D0370088

READING MODERN POETRY

READING
MODERN POETRY

Michael Schmidt

821.7/09
S353

R

ROUTLEDGE

London and New York

Alverno College
Library Media Center
Milwaukee, Wisconsin

First published 1989
by Routledge
11 New Fetter Lane, London EC4P 4EE
29 West 35th Street, New York, NY 10001

© 1989 Michael Schmidt

Disk conversion and composition by
Mayhew Typesetting, Bristol, UK
Printed in Great Britain by
Richard Clay Ltd, Bungay, Suffolk

All rights reserved. No part of this book may be
reprinted or reproduced or utilized in any form or
by any electronic, mechanical, or other means,
now known or hereafter invented, including
photocopying and recording, or in any
information storage or retrieval system, without
permission in writing from the publishers.

British Library Cataloguing in Publication Data
Schmidt, Michael,
Reading modern poetry
1. Poetry in English — Critical Studies
I. Title
821'.009

Library of Congress Cataloging in Publication Data
Schmidt, Michael,
Reading modern poetry/Michael Schmidt.
p. cm.
1. English poetry — 20th century — History and criticism.
2. Books and reading. I. Title.
PR601.S355 1989
821'.9109—dc20 89–6213

ISBN 0–415–01568–5 HB
0–415–01569–3 PB

For Victor Ross

The roses of irony blossom
floridly on the trellis
of inexperience crossed with
a need for the fell and certain.

Donald Davie, 'The Nosegay'

CONTENTS

Acknowledgements

The author and publishers are grateful to the following for permission to reproduce poems/extracts: Anvil Press Poetry Ltd for 'Irony and Love' by Dick Davis from *In the Distance* (1975) on p. 103; BBC Radio Collection for the extract from Radio 4 'Kaleidoscope' (*PN Reviews* 66, 1989) by Seamus Heaney on p. 96; Bloodaxe Books Ltd for 'Atlantis' by David Constantine from *Watching for Dolphins* (1983) on p. 19; Charles Causley/David Higham Associates for the extract from *Worlds* by Charles Causley (1974) on p. 39; Faber & Faber Ltd for the extracts from 'The True Confessions' by George Barker (1965) on p. 38 (UK rights only), from *Worlds* by Thom Gunn (1974) on p. 41 and by Seamus Heaney (1974) on p. 38, from 'Hugh Selwyn Mauberley' by Ezra Pound in *Collected Shorter Poems* (1968) on p. 86, and from 'Volcano' by Derek Walcott in *Collected Poems* (1988) on pp. 40 and 78–9; Mrs Nessie Graham for 'Johann Joachim Quantz's Five Lessons' by W. S. Graham from *Collected Poems* (Faber & Faber Ltd, 1980) on p. 13; Michael Hofmann for 'The Austrians after Sadowa (1866)' (1982) on p. 31; John Johnson (Authors' Agents) Ltd for the extract from 'The True Confessions' by George Barker (1965) on p. 38 (US rights only); Lawrence and Wishart Publishers for the extract by Dorothy Edwards from *Scrutinies by Various Writers* (1928) on pp. 35–6; Liveright Publishing Company for the extract by Hart Crane from *Complete Poems and Selected Letters* (1966) on p. 89; Edwin Morgan for his extract from *Worlds* (1974) on p. 37; New Directions Publishing Corporation for the extract from Ezra Pound's *Personae*, © 1926 Ezra Pound, (US rights only); Oxford University Press for 'On the Fly-Leaf of Pound's *Cantos*' © Basil Bunting, reprinted from Basil Bunting's *Collected Poems* (1978) on p. 117, and for the extract by Allen Tate from *Essays of Four Decades* (1970) on p. 20; Oxford University Press New Zealand for 'The Buried Stream' by James K. Baxter (1982) on p. 95, and for 'Time' by Mary Ursula Bethell from *Ursula Bethell Collected Poems* (1985) on p. 85; Peter Sansom for 'The Fox in the Writing Class' on p. 112, which will appear in the forthcoming Carcanet title *Everything You've Heard is True* (1990); The University of Tennessee Press for the extracts from *Czeslaw Milosz and the Insufficiency of the Lyric* (1986) by Donald Davie on pp. 43 and 62–3.

All sources other than those listed above or in the Reading List are courtesy of Carcanet Press Ltd.

1

Now we must try higher, aware of the terrible
Shapes of silence sitting outside your ear
Anxious to define you and really love you.
Remember silence is curious about its opposite
Element which you shall learn to represent.

W. S. Graham, 'Johann Joachim Quantz's Five Lessons'

Editors are very visible readers. Their enthusiasms, commitments and aberrations issue in books and magazines. They would be disingenuous to pretend that there is not a certain bias in their reading, the colouring of specific loyalties and prejudices.

I am a publisher, magazine editor and teacher, not a critic. Donald Davie called me a *vulgarisateur* – the French word sounds less harsh than its English equivalent. I think he is right. English poetry has been my chief interest for thirty years, but my grasp of critical theories and their ideologies is tenuous. Literary publishers are publishers because they are not writers. They are not even critics. They do what they take to be the next best thing. When I was invited to write this essay, it was as a publisher. I took my task to be a descriptive, not a theoretical one.

Some readers will say that this approach is itself ideological – quite as much as a Marxizing, feminist or post-structuralist approach would be. Terry Eagleton, a *vulgarisateur* of literary theory and a Protean Marxist, insists that 'Hostility to theory usually means an opposition to other people's theories and an oblivion of one's own.' I think this is too categorical, rather like Freud insisting that all dreams are wish fulfilments, and if your dream isn't a wish fulfilment, you wish to prove him wrong, so it is a wish fulfilment.

The theories that entertain whole University faculties, and the 'literature' of the theorists which is sometimes ambitious to displace the things it theorizes upon, tend to be *a priori*, to establish norms of reading and interpretation by which to approach poems and prose, and the struggle (it is a struggle) starts with trying to define what is meant by 'literature' itself. The Russian Formalists developed their theories out of reading specific poems and works of prose in a language remote from our own in tradition and construction. The conclusions they drew, the theories they evolved, are now abstracted from the texts they read and the languages they spoke and wrote and – in the world of vivid, half-grasped ideas, the world of under-graduate study for example – are 'popularized' in dozens of exegetical essays and books divorced from the very context that validates them.

When I was reading 'The Knight's Tale' in a university then noted for its conservative approach, I spent my time coming to terms with Chaucer's Middle English, his verse forms, the sources and analogues of the story and its place in the pattern of the *Canterbury Tales*. A friend of mine at Cambridge was reading the same text in the light of various theoretical approaches. When we talked about the poem, his reading was remote from mine. Certain lines and single words were packed with significance for him which, for me, had seemed part of the wonderfully even distribution of sense that Chaucer (like Spenser) achieves. My friend's readings displaced the intellec-tual and formal climaxes of the poem. If it is unwise to trust the teller, not the tale, surely (it appeared to me) it was as risky to come at a poem with too clear a sense of what one intended to find. A maxim for our time might be: *never trust the critic, trust the tale*.

If I accept Terry Eagleton's axiom and confess to an informing ideology, a theory reluctant to dignify itself with what seems to it a spurious title, I cannot say whether that theory is radical or conservative. It appears radical in one sense: much of the best writing of our century seems both to have been and still to be overlooked and suppressed, and some of the greatest pleasures in modern poetry are uncharted ones. On the other hand, it appears conservative because I believe that reading modern poetry entails an understanding 'on the pulse' of the poetry of the past, and therefore a willing self-effacement before challenging new work. My theory is wary of generalizations about the creative process, about the ways in which the language of poetry relates to the social and natural worlds, or the ways in which the words in the poem relate to one another.

Philip Larkin and W. S. Graham, for example, are poets very different in character: they use language in contrasting ways, they approach form from opposite directions, they have a distinct regard (and disregard) for their audience. Their sense of the natural and social worlds, and the ways language touches upon and draws from them, could hardly be more disparate. They must be read in rather different ways. Except for analytical techniques proposed by some of the linguistic critics, I have found no theory useful apart from a conventional theory of tradition and canon, which accommodates both Larkin and Graham together, granting them, within a common language, a common patrimony to which they contribute, which they extend in their own ways. Poetry is a collaborative art, and yet – as it is being created – the most solitary and 'individual' of activities.

The American poet Allen Tate had a name for this kind of theory. He called it 'aesthetic-historical'. He was reluctant to limit the word 'aesthetic' to anything more specific than 'a mode of perception', 'a heightened sensitivity'. Thus attenuated, and qualified by the word 'historical' – not in a determinist or Marxizing sense but to indicate context and occasion – 'aesthetic' gains a degree of muscle and becomes serviceable.

I believe that readers come to poetry; poetry which sets out to buttonhole readers can be vitiated by the compromises it makes. It sometimes patronizes its audience and plays at entertainment. The pleasure that the best poetry gives is different from 'entertainment'. It is a pleasure of enhancement and extension, and it can be a durable pleasure if the poem finds its way into memory. There are ways of popularizing the presentation of poetry, but the art itself cannot be simplified without damage.

One of the best public performers of his own work, Tony

Harrison, takes great pains to explain the difficult allusions in his poems before he performs them, to outline the occasion out of which they came, and to leaven the performance with jokes. He prepares the audience, and the poems come across even to those who have not read them before. But his skill at presentation is unusual. Other poets who regularly perform their work in public can – as Robert Lowell says he did – begin to simplify the texture of the poem as they recite it, to leave out hard bits, to change the syntax, to translate Latin tags and difficult words: in short, to compromise the written text. When it came time for Lowell to reprint some of the poems he had performed most often, he found himself revising them in the light of his recitals. He developed a habit of rewriting earlier poems, even changing their forms and rhythms. The written text became unstable as a result of the adjustments and compromises with audiences that he found himself making – out of a kind of misplaced courtesy, perhaps. Lowell is not the only poet who responded to the demands of audiences in this way. There is no denying the benefits of public recitals for audiences; but we should not overlook the effect that repeated public performances have on poets.

I take it for granted that there is a canon of English language poetry which relates to other classical and modern canons. Poets find their bearings from an understanding (or a creative misunderstanding) of elements in those canons, and *reading* poetry involves taking bearings from them as well.

In reading new poems it is necessary to develop certain senses, the most important being a sense of tradition. To understand almost by second nature how certain forms, dictions, conventions and genre have developed in English writing and to hear how they are reshaped in new work is an essential talent; to listen for allusion, interplay, influence and rhyme within the tradition – those subtle, surprising echoes that electrify, for example, some of the poems of Geoffrey Hill, or W. S. Graham, or Stevie Smith.

We should not confuse these senses – or second-senses – which develop over years of committed reading with the analytical skills which any student can master. 'Reading skills':

the phrase smacks of blackboards and exercise books. Skilled readers know just what to look for. They know the technical terms and can count metrical feet on their fingers. Some poets – I have W. S. Graham particularly in mind – rail at readers of this kind. Graham's test for those admirers who visited him at his home in Madron, near Penzance, was to make them read his poems aloud. He would approve or remonstrate, even on occasion 'correct' them. The human voice (the reader's, not the poet's) was the first and most incisive critical instrument. It betrayed comprehension and incomprehension. That is how close a sensitive reader stands to the poem. He may find it hard to talk about it, but he knows how it works because of the way it has moved his tongue and lips, has worked on and in him.

2

It dies hard, the notion of a just people;
  The wish that there should have been once mutual
    aid
Dies very hard. Through fire, through ghastly ash and
    any
  Smothering weight of water still we imagine
A life courteous and joyful; see them lightly clad
  Loving the sun, the vine and the grey olive.
Over the water, from trading, they come home winged
  With sails, their guide and harbinger the white dove.

David Constantine, 'Atlantis'

We can respond readily enough, at a certain level, to the poetry of our own time. But assessing it is hard. Time is a great – though not a final – winnower. When we pick up a book of poems by a writer whose work we do not know, we meet peculiarities of language – diction or syntax, formal structure or metre – which may be the product of technical inadequacies or of excessive competence; or they have a deeper source which we must intuit and engage tentatively, with risk if we try to translate our intuition into a prose statement. Some of the potent and memorable poetry of our time appears at first to be a language of concealment. The 'occasion' for a poem may be so intimate and difficult that it issues in tantalizing imagery and complex syntax which appear to be out of keeping with the theme. Perhaps the poet is not *saying* anything at all: he may be conveying a tone, a mood, or enacting a process of feeling.

Perhaps he has set out to say something which the poem will not let him say – the way that Marvell in his great 'An Horatian Ode upon Cromwell's Return from Ireland' found it impossible not to balance the celebratory occasion with the underlying and darker truth of that occasion, the king's execution. In Philip Larkin's 'Church Going', the poem says much more than the 'bored, uninformed' speaker seems to intend: the wry closing line fails to undercut the superb affirmation of the final stanza. Many a poem of celebration strikes an elegiac note; some poems on political themes cannot make the statement the poet intends, not because of a failure of nerve on the poet's part but because of the corrective force of the poetic form chosen, the demands it makes on the *whole* imagination, and the qualifications inherent in any achieved poem.

Allen Tate raises the larger issue in these terms:

> The difference between Pound's 'Mauberley' and Arnold's 'Obermann' is not merely a difference of diction or subject; it is the subtle difference between two ways of trying to get out of history what Herbert or Crashaw would have expected only from God. Both Arnold and Pound are asking history to make them whole – Arnold through philosophy, Pound through art, or aesthetic sensibility; and unless this difference is grasped the critic will pull himself up short at the mere differences of 'style'.   (*Essays of Four Decades*: 217–18)

This relates to much British poetry since the Second World War, and especially to writers who have come of age since the War. For the majority of poets of my generation – those between the ages of 30 and 50 – religious verities are not only untenable but remote, hardly capable of imaginative engagement. Biblical incidents and characters may be alluded to, but in the way that classical gods and legends are. The contrast between the generation of R. S. Thomas, C. H. Sisson, George Barker, and John Heath-Stubbs – poets in their seventies – and that of Jeffrey Wainwright, Tom Paulin, Carol Rumens, Jeremy Hooker, and John Ash could hardly be more pronounced. And in the intervening generation there are poets such as Philip Larkin and, in a different spirit, Geoffrey Hill, who have Thomas Hardy's hunger for faith, or Ted Hughes whose religious repudiations in *Crow* are eloquent, or Donald Davie who gnaws insistently at what he takes to be the essential skeleton of our culture, the Anglican and Dissenting traditions. There has been so complete a change of key, a secularization of imagination in my generation, that the impact upon the art is undeniable. It affects approaches to audience and theme, and consequently to questions of form and language.

It is hard not to see 1968 as a poetic, quite as much as a political, watershed. When, in the early 1970s, C. H. Sisson addressed my students at Manchester University, he was questioned about his poem 'The Usk'. His insistence on the Incarnation and all that – surely it was just a matter of opinion. Sisson 'struck the board' and reminded us that for a Christian the Incarnation is a matter of fact. For a poet who is a Christian it is the sacramental ground of his imagination. A failure or loss of belief entails the loss of that sustaining fact. Absence of belief is another matter: questions of truth arise in quite other terms for the poets of my generation.

Many of the younger British poets turn to history for subject matter, theme and consolation. Though the short lyric poem has not been cast out, it has taken on a rather different value for them than it had for Graves, or Dylan Thomas, or Larkin. The sequence of lyrics, or the pseudo-sequence, has come into its own. Where Thomas Hardy arranged the poems in his collections in such a way as to emphasize contrast and variety, contemporary poets generally try to create 'integrated' collections.

The grudging praise for the poems of accomplished writers such as Dick Davis and Robert Wells, whose work insists upon and proves the continued validity of the traditional lyric mode, is a symptom of something that runs deeper than fashion, something closely related to the tentative culture of the day and the ideologies that at once underpin and subvert it.

Certainly the poetic sequence on an historical theme, running to middle length (anything from 80 to 400 lines), with specific strategies and objectives, has come into its own in the last twenty years. Geoffrey Hill's *Mercian Hymns* is the most complex and radical poem of this kind; his later, in some ways more conventional major poem, *The Mystery of the Charity of Charles Péguy*, and the early 'Funeral Music' sequence are central to the development. Such sequences draw upon history but do not set out to recount it. Poetic wholeness is achieved by fragmentation of a narrative line or lines (history, legend,

21

biography, autobiography) taken as given, and then built upon with certain interpolations and omissions.

For Hill the sequences are genuinely historical and cultural: he is not bending history and legend to serve the present. Make It Real, not Make It New. Other poets have used rather than served their chosen historical themes, finding in them an oblique way of writing about the present. Hill insists on the presence of the past, the abiding qualities in a culture or a life. He is scrupulous in his use of fact: if Péguy is relevant to us today, that relevance inheres in who and what he was, in the quality of his life, his rootedness in the old France, his vexed radicalism, his troubled Christianity, his intractability: he is exemplary from where he fell in a beetroot field on the first day of the first battle of the Marne; Hill tries not to traduce him into the 1980s or to give him a factitious relevance. Hill is incapable of sentimentalizing events or characters.

Younger writers have learned from Hill, though none possess his rigour. The theme of Enclosure has attracted poets whose natural inclination was to the pastoral yet whose sense of history and politics made it impossible for them to adopt without irony and obliquity the traditional pastoral modes. Andrew Motion's first ambitious sequence, 'Inland', a Newdigate Prize poem at Oxford, dramatizes and elegizes a remote time and allows the reader to draw political corollaries from the lives it portrays. 'Independence', a later poem, more subtly draws on the lattermath of the Raj. Motion's natural idiom and sensibility are those of a lyric poet, but he was wary of the stable lyric voice: the elegiac pressure was great, while the sense of single occasion was not sufficiently strong to govern him, until latterly.

Jeremy Hooker took as his first enabling image the Cerne Abbas chalk giant in Dorset and made a sequence out of its presence and its mystery. The Giant becomes a kind of tutelary being for him, a focal point, a spirit of place. *Place* is his dominant concern. David Day wrote a sequence about brass rubbing: it's a matter of touching, feeling, intuiting the past from artefacts, discovering the elements of which one is oneself made, elements which history has eroded and tarnished, devalued and unmade, but not quite destroyed. In the sequences the poet approaches the same tangle of themes again and again from different angles, attempting to unravel and clarify them.

A poet who took his bearings quite directly from Geoffrey Hill is Jeffrey Wainwright. In his most celebrated poem, a sequence of twelve connected lyrics, each consisting of three unrhymed triplets, he elects Thomas Muntzer, the sixteenth-century Protestant reformer – 'a radical and a visionary both in theology and politics for whom religious thought and experience became integrated with ideas and movements towards social revolution' – as the vehicle for his exploration of political concerns of our own time, the late 1960s and early 1970s. He is drawn not to the integrated vision of the theology of Muntzer's story but to the politics. He plants himself in Muntzer's situation, fuses himself imaginatively with the reformer and brings what seem to be details of his own life into play (rather as Geoffrey Hill does in sections of *Mercian Hymns*). The poem sidesteps the religious theme, or translates it out of theology, and yet it is instinct with a kind of unattenuated political understanding – of a quality which inheres in this difficult form, suspended between narrative, dramatic monologue, and moral exemplum, and would have eluded Wainwright had he approached his concerns less obliquely, more in the terms of his own day. Here again one senses a natural hunger for a pastoral mode which is no longer tenable. There is an echo too of Langland (and the Bible) in the attempt at social comprehensiveness, as in the seventh section which expresses an ideal the poem exists at once to validate and (by taking its theme from history) to show defeated:

> He teaches the gardener from his trees
> And the fisherman from his catch, even
> The goldsmith from the testing of his gold.
>
> In the pond the cold thick water clothes me.
> I live with the timorous snipe, beetles
> And skaters, the pike smiles and moves with me.

We hold it in common without jealousy.
Touch your own work and the simple world.
In these unread creatures sings the real gospel.
                            ('Thomas Muntzer')

The phrase 'the real gospel' seems to appropriate to the essentially political (or historical) the authority that Muntzer himself would have attributed to God. History – and anachronism. This is not finally poetry as re-enactment or re-possession of historical truths but a poetry of historical displacement.

Sequences which mingle voices and dramatize situations, disrupted poetic narratives, streams of consciousness, oblique biographies which appropriate figures and make them talk at a distance about present realities: in such work the voice, the lyric 'I', is attenuated. The poet wishes not so much to speak as to speak for. If there is a major modernist behind these strategies it is not Pound or Eliot or even Yeats, but Joyce. No masked first person speaks, but a ventriloquist.

Such poems set out to be responsible statement. There was little space in a world as serious as the late 1960s and early 1970s seemed to be for the indulgence of the mere first person. When the first person is used it is for the most part either with a defined moral severity or in a spirit of self-parody and irony. This creating a distance between the poem and the poet is the essence of irony, but different in effect – deliberately so – from the ironies of the poets associated with the Movement of the 1950s, whose reaction against the afflatus of the louder writers of the 1940s was to chasten and contain poetry in recognizable forms and to accentuate the element of craft. For them irony is more a stylistic than a strategic instrument. It is the social element in 'voice', not an escape from it.

For Alison Brackenbury the historical occasion may be a Tudor lady (*Dreams of Power*) or John Clare (*Breaking Ground*). Her sequences too are lyrical in spirit, they too retain the dew of the pastoral, and yet their impulse is elegiac and, in a very real sense, political. Here too metaphysics are kept at bay: the visions open into nature (human and otherwise) and not through it on to larger verities or blinding voids. Brackenbury has found her way back to the lyric in her most recent writing, yet even those lyric poems are arranged in 'runs' which seek to work as a sequence.

Val Warner in *Before Lunch*, a long, ambitious product of a kind of sensibility common to younger writers of the 1970s, orchestrates voices and characters in an almost-present, playing snatches of song, social and media clichés, vulgar journalism, literary allusion, and lived anguish, over one another. The lyric voice is again unstable, untenable, yet out of the babble of registers, none finally the poet's own, emerges a tone – if not of voice, then of feeling. Warner is among the few British poets for whom the pastoral has ceased to be even a residual resource.

If one takes the sequences of James Fenton, starting with his Newdigate Prize poem 'Our Western Furniture', about the opening of Japan to the west, and following on to the (in my view) major achievement of 'A German Requiem', one again sees how a strategy of 'historical indirection' can yield a poetry that is compellingly direct. In a language almost devoid of metaphor and decoration, a language which mimes the deliberate, 'official' forgetting of a past not by an individual but by a society, a vital political statement is enacted. Such poetry is effective: it does not convince, it persuades.

The same can be said of some of the poems in Tony Harrison's *Continuous* sequence and of some of his longer poems. It's not that he eschews the first person, far from it; but he is a poet whose very social mobility away from class and regional antecedents has been by means of languages, so that he is a veritable Pentecost, speaking in tongues and trying to give voice to many dictions and idioms which a dominant culture (in his view) has deliberately ignored or suppressed. Class conflict in his poems has a rather 1930s feel about it, though he has ambitiously tried to approach head-on the conflicts of contemporary Britain – including the problems of racism – in his controversial poem '*v*'. His chief advantage is, perhaps, his training in dramatic writing and translation and, as I have said, the virtuosity with which he performs his poems. His politics too are poetically potent because they are enacted

25

in appropriate languages, through anecdote or historical event. He has the range and grasp – and something of the repetitive rhythmic and moral insistence – of Kipling, though his household gods are Milton and Keats.

Few of his contemporaries (an undervalued generation including figures of stature such as Ken Smith, Brian Jones, Peter Scupham, Rodney Pybus, and Alistair Elliot) strive for his immediacy. Ken Smith would seem to be an exception, but he seldom achieves the balance (often arrived at through humour) that marks the best of Harrison's poems, and he lacks the coarse richness of texture in the language. Peter Scupham's language is brilliantly textured but never coarse: elegant, scholarly, refined, his voice is not 'public' enough, though his themes are. Brian Jones lacks Harrison's ventriloquist skills and his attractive social credentials. He does not share Scupham's erudite and very natural way with traditional forms. But he has emerged as a poet impatient of obliquity at a time when British political life seems to him to be in crisis, and his sequences of personal and political poems – set in classical or modern times – have urgency and a rare prophetic seriousness about them.

Why is this not an age of satire? Partly, no doubt, because of the absence of consensus in the community, of shared values, the absence of social and moral stability which provide the necessary ground for satire. Partly, too, because satire requires a single-mindedness from the poet which is rare nowadays. There are of course satirists, but their verse is merely topical. And the poet who wishes to get direct purchase on his present political world faces the perennial problem of dating or dated allusion – a problem we experience when we read *The Hind and the Panther* or *The Dunciad* or those satires of the 1930s, whose incidents and heroes have been buried by history or apathy. It is a problem Donald Davie identifies in his poem 'Remembering the 'Thirties' (*Collected Poems*, 1972):

> This novel written fifteen years ago,
> Set in my boyhood and my boyhood home,
> These poems about 'abandoned workings', show
> Worlds more remote than Ithaca or Rome.

The Anschluss, Guernica – all the names
At which those poets thrilled or were afraid
For me mean schools and schoolmasters and games;
And in the process some-one is betrayed.

Ourselves perhaps. The Devil for a joke
Might carve his own initials on our desk,
And yet we'd miss the point because he spoke
An idiom too dated, Audenesque.

Satire is less viable today than it was in the 1950s, unless the satirist is preaching to the converted. The force of a savage satire like Edgell Rickword's 1937 'To the Wife of a Non-Interventionist Statesman' derives from the poet's human outrage at the bombing of Guernica and his conviction that he shares common moral ground with others who might not accept his political views. It also derives from a close reading of Swift and other great English satirists, and it realizes its radical politics in the particulars it evokes.

Euzkadi's mines supply the ore
to feed the Nazi dogs of war:
Guernica's thermite rain transpires
in doom on Oxford's dreaming spires:
in Hitler's frantic mental haze
already Hull and Cardiff blaze,
and Paul's grey dome rocks to the blast
of air-torpedoes screaming past.
From small beginnings mighty ends,
from calling rebel generals friends,
from being taught at public schools
to think the common people fools,
Spain bleeds, and England wildly gambles
to bribe the butcher in the shambles.

If more poets read Dryden, Swift, and Pope – *read* them rather than studied them – satire might regain its vigour and earn itself a new audience. There is no lack of angry writers around today, and not a few poems are written for use in public halls where the performer can count upon a sympathetic reception.

But for those poets who are not by nature preachers, even though they may have a very defined politics, 'a neutral tone is nowadays preferred'. Few even of the poets who have the formal competence for satirical writing are confident of a shared moral ground with their readers – or confident, indeed, of their readers.

The poets of the 1950s got by, imagining that the common reader still existed somewhere, and perhaps he did. Perhaps he still does, but in such a diaspora that the poet has only the vaguest sense of his presence. Little wonder then that the oblique historical strategy seeks out events and characters from the past parallel or adaptable to current concerns. Poets resort to them – especially if they are distanced from the class or community they attempt to speak for or with – in order to celebrate common struggle, lament common loss, when they cannot engage directly with the immediate world and when they are uncomfortable with the first person singular.

This all stems from a problem of audience, to be sure, and from the estrangement of the community from its poets or vice versa. It is also a problem of language. There is a language of enactment (in the liturgy, 'With this ring I thee wed') and a language of description ('I give you this ring as a symbol of our marriage'). The first is a language of faith (not necessarily a religious faith: it can be a firm sense of a given world in which qualities inhere) while the second is a language attenuated and distanced from the things it names, a language which finds conviction hard and works by deliberate symbolism, by the attribution rather than the embodiment of values and qualities.

And that is the language of much modern poetry; at best it is convinced that belief is out of place, that in a world of relativities a language of defined personality and display, an ironic mode and a wry dispassion are tolerable modes. Some find it preferable to abandon 'self' in service of 'larger themes'. Few endorse (or practise) a poetry that talks barefaced. The element that distinguishes poets such as Iain Crichton Smith, Seamus Heaney, Les A. Murray, and Derek Walcott is an insistence on the validity of the first person singular which, if sometimes it resorts to ironies, does so because those ironies are part of a 'literal' voice, not of a carefully constructed persona. None of these writers is English – they are a Scot, an Irishman, an Australian and a poet from the Caribbean. For the contemporary English writer, irony is almost inescapable. It is a national tic, a vice, a voice no longer confined to the middle classes.

In the distinctive writing of poets whose vocation developed in the 1960s there is a degree of moral tentativeness even when the poem seems most urgently to address moral issues. There is a failure of transcendence, even of hunger for transcendence. 'Voice' is valued by critics as something that sets poets apart and individuates them, rather than the Wordsworthian 'voice' which was a heightening of common language and a sharpening of common experience. The eccentric and offbeat are the market-makers; if performance skills combine with eccentricity, so much the better. Academic wit has never been so much in vogue as it is today. Its most successful manifestation is in the work of the so-called Martian group.

Against such trends can be set the challenging work of poets associated with the name of J. H. Prynne. They resist the age, decline commercial publication and exposure of the kind which they believe would distort or compromise their work. They harbour no illusions about readership, general or otherwise. Diverse in their approaches, they share with the poets described here a penchant for poetic sequences; the term 'lyric' does not detain them for long. Survivors of academic training (largely at Cambridge), they need for their work a criticism that will level the approach for new readers – for theirs strikes me as a poetry that will not be received without a deliberately conceived and fundamental adjustment of poetic intelligence in this country. The challenge they offer can seem more of a hygiene than a pleasure, yet they stand against the passive conventionality and the general intellectual poverty of the day. They are in the wings – not waiting to perform a coup on the establishment, but working.

3

They live as well as they can – the irony
of a small people living in a small country
that was once an empire, with its own navy
and foreign policy, administration and style.
In this century of their loss, they have had
more than their share of innovators; dominating
in philosophy, science, psychology, the arts. . .
After the death of power, the lightning of analysis.

Michael Hofmann, 'The Austrians after Sadowa (1866)'

If a census was taken, it would reveal that well over half the published contemporary poets under the age of fifty are employed in educational establishments at secondary or tertiary level, or derive a substantial part of their income from those sources in some form. These writer–teachers are not to be confused with Coleridge's leavening clerisy, vocational servants bringing from the citadels of learning a culture, a set of values into the community, though some might see their vocation in that light. For the institutions in which they serve (especially if they bear a title like 'Resident Poet' or 'Fellow of Poetry') they are talismans of cultural commitment, tolerated and advertised as such. A Poet in Residence is proof of creative patronage, a nod in the direction of Living Culture. He can absolve the host institution of many sins. It is not wrong that poets should eat or that houses of learning should set a table for them. I am merely reflecting on a fact of poetic life in Britain today. In the United States it has become virtually *the* fact of poetic life.

An intimate relationship with the educational establishment – amounting to dependence upon it – and a continual engagement with students and teaching colleagues who are the civil servants in the Republic of Letters, must affect writers rather more than a job in the City, the Forces or a trade would do. Not since the decline of Court patronage have so many poets belonged to one profession. And as a profession it encourages certain approaches to language, audience and criticism. 'Professing' and teaching are not inevitably homogenizing or reductive roles for a poet; but it would be short-sighted not to note that certain critical strategies affect creative effort, and the production of texts suitable for exegesis at various levels is allied to manufacture more closely than it it is to the old divine afflatus, or the play and the truth-telling of untrammeled spirits. Certain fashions – in political preference, formal disposition and the like – characterize different levels and institutions of learning. A poet who is too closely watched, too indiscriminately admired, too protected, is likely to become a performer.

The desire of writers to 'become literature', themselves to feature in anthologies or on the general syllabus, is an affliction from which some of my contemporaries suffer. I admire C. H. Sisson's observation, that the avoidance of literature is essential to the man who would tell the truth. This is not so much an axiom as an observation in the context of an essay on the nineteenth-century Dorset poet William Barnes. As Robert Frost insisted time after time, Shakespeare was never sacred to himself (though Frost may have been). The poet eager for posterity, especially the chalk-dust posterity of the classroom and lecture hall, will find himself playing to an audience of literary critics and curriculum advisers, a demanding audience in one way, but rather a narrow one in another.

'You always read poetry through poetry', one of my students told me accusingly. Yes, I believe it is the first way to read poetry. But it does not imply reading poetry according to the various orthodoxies of academic practice, or sacralizing the art in seminar rooms with earnest discussion, or writing essays, or privately digesting the critical and theoretical opinions of other readers, even if they are critics. These are strictly valueless if the poems they address have not been read, and read carefully. Poems are 'literature' only when they are on the shelf or when they are being written about by critics or read about by students. Taken down, approached without ulterior motive, *read* on the page, they are released from that dusty category.

Other considerations follow. The habit of reading poems for their propriety of thought, their usefulness to particular critical strategies or 'theories', the light they cast on an age, is common. It can be reductive. It can lead to undervaluing Milton, Shelley, and Pound or to exaggerating the claims of Clare, Owen, and MacNeice on our attention.

In 1936 W. H. Auden declared that 'the commonest cause of badness in any of the arts is being really interested in one subject while pretending to be interested in another.' That seems a proper caution: one can read Milton for his politics or Herbert for his theology, but that exercise is not necessarily the same as reading the poetry of Milton or Herbert.

One can compare the early and later work of Adrienne Rich and see how her radical analysis of language, form and the nature of poetic statement have changed her art, and from this one can draw conclusions about the feminist enterprise; but if one is concerned with the poems – as statement or process – one will not reject the early poems in favour of the later. Even when poems are offered for use by a cause, as in protest poetry, they should still be available to readers *as* poems. Poetry if it must preach preaches best to the unconverted. George Herbert writes towards communion, not after it; his prayers create a space into which an answer can come, but they do not propose the answer.

What poets do with form, metre, diction and metaphor; the spaces they create in feeling by an art which they have mastered; how their work engages their world and the world, their time and the timeless: these things are of more interest than their opinions, philosophies and theologies, or politics. The poet Burns Singer wrote:

> Thought is always and only thought.
> The thinking's different. Thinking's in the blood.

Poetry is process, a 'form of discovery', which, if it serves a cause, transcends it. Otherwise the unbeliever could hardly approach Dante or Milton, Herbert or Hopkins; and the political conservative (along with some radicals) would recoil from Blake, Shelley, and MacDiarmid.

Edgell Rickword wrote of John Donne in 1924:

> The faculty which distinguishes the noblest poets from the interesting majority of writers and artists is the gift of perceiving the universe, not through the disparate evidence of the senses or through the conceptual entities of the intelligence, but as a unity in which all the dualisms are extinguished. But once the evidence for the possession of this gift has been received we are not to demand that the poet shall testify incessantly to a unity, 'like an angel out of a cloud', which manifestly is not an attribute of human experience. Rather we should be glad that he descends to illuminate the dualistic world in which we pass much of our time; and it is then a delightful task of aesthetic criticism to reveal the form and pattern of the poet's creation. For it is this aesthetic whole, the poem concrete in rhythm, rhyme and imagery, which, whatever its subject, constitutes the body in which and through which we can perceive the idea of beauty.
>
> (*Essays and Opinions 1921–1931*: 19)

The words 'noblest' and 'beauty' date the essay but they do not invalidate it. 'Noblest' is more serviceable than 'greatest', 'best' or 'major', suggesting as it does the qualities of spirit, range and moral worth which have little to do with the *bourse* of reputations, much to do with older traditions. And the word 'beauty' as defined by its context here is not a romantic vacuity but something very specific which has to do with the character of poetic synthesis and harmony, even in works which are not conventionally harmonious. At the heart of Rickword's argument is the realism of the practitioner – for he was a fine poet himself – which recognizes that a writer cannot be expected consistently to achieve the highest 'testimony'.

Rickword became one of the defining critics of his time, writing the first book in English on the French poet Arthur Rimbaud, reviewing 'The Waste Land' in *The Times Literary Supplement* with remarkable astuteness when it appeared in 1922, and justly assessing not only the best writing of the past but new talents as they came to light. He started the 'Scrutinies' which revised the reputations of writers misvalued by fashion

and the taste-makers of the day. His later political radicalism was insistently particular, so that the literary essays he
wrote when he became a Communist in the 1930s and after
retain their value today for curious readers of any political
kidney. There is a passage in the Foreword to Rickword's
first anthology of *Scrutinies* which makes sense in this
context:

> Nor does it seem correct, though it is often suggested, that
> criticism of contemporary work can never be so 'pure' as that
> of a thoroughly dead subject. But it is a critic's business to
> evaluate his own temporal bias just as he would an historical
> qualification; and if it had not been so frequently assumed
> that a critic who cannot deal intelligently with a contem-
> porary becomes, by some queer metamorphosis, intelligent
> when discussing a classic, literary history would not have
> become the dust-bin it is.
>
> (*Essays and Opinions 1921–1931*: 275–6)

This was written in 1928, at a time when modern poetry had
not been dignified with inclusion in any secondary school
syllabus and was still less than 'established' as a University
subject. It was before there was a targetable poetry market but
a readership still existed, committed and conservative, quite
capable of buying up thousands of copies of a favourite contemporary – John Masefield, say – and expressing violent indigna-
tion about the modern. It was the autumn of the pastoral mode
(but then it is still the autumn of the pastoral mode in British
poetry, and perhaps it always will be). Satire was not thriving.
Narrative poetry was being attempted. Dorothy Edwards wrote
in her 'Scrutiny' of G. K. Chesterton:

> He cannot describe this world in anything but paradoxes, the
> outward sign of something changing into something else. If
> he cannot demonstrate to you that absolutely everything here
> is miraculous, he will try to deceive you by his manner, and
> solemnly tell you that it is a miracle that grass is green or that
> 'the daisy has a ring of red.' This last bit of information is so
> wonderful that

In the last wreck of Nature dark and dread
Shall, in eclipse's hideous hieroglyph,
One wild form reel on the last rocking cliff
And shout. . .

it. But he can indeed look at anything with the eyes of a child
and find it unfamiliar. We do not question his success at the
game, we only question its value. . . . The hero of this world
is of course the man who walks on his hands because walk-
ing on his feet is too unexciting, who enters his house
through the chimney, who plays an unexpected and
perpetual game of hide and seek with his wife; its singer is
the poet whose verse 'sprawls like the trees, dances like the
dust, is ragged like the thundercloud, top-heavy like the
toadstool.'   (*Scrutinies by Various Writers*: 35–6)

Well, it was a different world sixty years ago, and yet the case
so lucidly made against Chesterton's 'classic' status (and its
effect on public expectations and on younger writers) is a case
that needs making in rather similar terms both in the academy
and in the *bourse* against the 'ludic' fashions of our day, where
the *frisson* of *daring to write* on painful or obscene subjects, or of
degrading a given physical or moral reality by a technique of
flashy, far-fetched metaphor (what critics like to call
'defamiliarizing' objects), or playing at extreme experience,
have created expectations among readers which have little to do
with poetry, much to do with the poet, journalism, and
academic wit. The product is personalized and marketed in the
light of the projected personality.

4

One could abandon writing
for the slow-burning signals
of the great, to be, instead
their ideal reader, ruminative,
voracious, making the love of masterpieces
superior to attempting
to repeat or outdo them,
and be the greatest reader in the world.

Derek Walcott, 'Volcano'

Good and great readers of poetry develop rather as poets do. An early fascination with words – nursery rhymes, football chants, hymns, advertisement jingles, ballads, pop-songs, or maybe words of the liturgy or the Bible – takes root in them. The Scottish poet Edwin Morgan has said:

There is a poetry before poetry – that is what I seem to see if I look back to my boyhood. . . . the imagination of someone who is going to write poetry can be stirred in all sorts of preparatory ways – through popular songs, through nature, through prose, through visual images, through knowledge.

(*Worlds*: 229)

He remembers his uncle singing popular songs of the day at the piano; his father's description during a Sunday walk of how steel was made; looking through 'a Victorian volume of my grandmother's filled with engravings of storms, wrecks and exotic atolls and icebergs,' and so on.

Seamus Heaney recalls early chants ('scurrilous and sectarian'), which were his initiation in Northern Ireland: 'They constitute a kind of poetry, not very respectable perhaps, but very much alive on the lips of that group of schoolboys. . . .' He had to memorize poetry at school but this was less vital to him.

The literary language, the civilised utterance from the classic canon of English poetry, was a kind of force-feeding. It did not delight us by reflecting our experience; it did not re-echo our own speech in formal and surprising arrangements. Poetry lessons, in fact, were rather like catechism lessons: official inculcations of hallowed formulae that were somehow expected to stand us in good stead in the adult life that stretched out ahead. (*Worlds*: 94)

There was also 'the recitation' which registered with him more directly than Poetry Lessons. He underwent the course, but grew more responsive to the range of English poetry later on.

George Barker was reading Byron at the age of 9. At 15 it was Eliot and Joyce and, more pertinently, Empson who had taken hold of him. He anchored his reading (and his art) in them. In his poem 'The True Confessions' he says:

> Track any poet to a beginning
> And in a dark room you discover
> A little boy intent on sinning
> With an etymological lover.

There was never anything systematic in his patterns of reading, of acquisition, but he became in his way learned.

Readers, like poets, can be trained only up to a certain point. Then something sparks an enthusiasm that transforms a text, a string of words, rhythms and rhymes, into a poem. They grow ardent. They move through a series of initially accidental encounters, until they experience a hunger that gives them direction, they take control of their reading. They may follow particular poets, learning from poems and from suggestions in their prose writings. They may seek out trustworthy critics for guidance. Good teachers, elder brothers and sisters, parents and friends give pointers, the way Siegfried Sassoon helped Wilfred Owen or Arthur Hallam helped Tennyson, or at a more radical level Wordsworth helped Coleridge (and vice versa). In our own time such creative relationships, starting at various points in poets' careers, are common: Donald Davie and Charles Tomlinson, David Wright and C. H. Sisson, Burns

Singer and W. S. Graham, Philip Larkin and Kingsley Amis, Sylvia Plath and Ted Hughes, Derek Walcott and Seamus Heaney.

Good reading is first a matter of controlling and then of soliciting the jolts and elations of new verbal experience. It becomes a question of deliberate and passionate extension. Some good readers are good critics, but not all critics are good readers and not all readers are able to justify their taste and judgement by critical argument.

'I think I became a working poet the day I joined the destroyer *Eclipse* at Scapa Flow in August, 1940', Charles Causley has written.

> From the moment I joined my first ship, I was spellbound by the sailors' lingo: about 500 basic words, about 495 of which I had never heard before. It was as full of poetry as the speech of Shakespeare's England. . . . Returning to Cornwall after the war, I saw its sights, heard its sounds and echoes, its forms of speech, as though I had been newly born.
>
> (*Worlds*: 23)

The art of reading, like that of writing, requires perspective, establishing a certain distance from one's own language, one's own concerns, even one's own community or country – in the way that irony can establish a gap between the speaker and what is being said, and in that gap exists our freedom to respond and discriminate. For Basil Bunting the distance was found in long exile – on the Continent, in contact with Yeats and Pound, with sullen diplomats and ambitious military officers in Persia – and in his pacifism during the Second World War. For Donald Davie the distance was provided by naval service in the War and the opportunity to learn Russian and assimilate elements of Slavic culture. Exile outside or within the community appears to be a common feature in the development of most of the significant poets of our time. That exile may be a spate of mental illness, a painful class adjustment, a teaching assignment in Prague, Khartoum, or Texas. It may, more simply, be a rejection of the poetic fashions and conventions of the day, a decision to stand apart.

It may be an encounter with prose. Charles Causley remembers the early impact of reading *David Copperfield*. And some lumps of Scott and Tennyson stuck in his mind from school. And hymns: especially Baring-Gould's 'Now the day is over'. 'The contents of *Hymns Ancient and Modern* printed themselves on my mind; and so did the songs I heard sung by the ex-soldiers who had survived the First World War.' The rhythms and stanza shapes of hymns also lodged themselves in his imagination, along with some of the darker themes, though not the plain man's theology that inheres in the Anglican hymn tradition.

Another poet, C. H. Sisson, stresses the accidental nature of his early development as reader and poet.

> The beginnings of poetry are hopelessly imitative, and it is difficult to see how the gathering burden could unload itself in rhymes which were nothing but John Drinkwater or Robert Louis Stevenson. But that was how the ecstasy in the coal-house ended when, later, I pressed my heart against the edge of the table and wrote the lines which appeared in the Children's Corner of the *Bristol Observer*.
>
> It is no doubt the inadequacy of the vehicle that makes one discard one's models with fury one after the other. John Drinkwater gave way to Rupert Brooke, Rupert Brooke to Edith Sitwell and to Dante Gabriel Rossetti. Finally John Drinkwater and Robert Louis Stevenson had to get out of the house, it shamed me so to see them on the shelves. . .
>
> (*The Avoidance of Literature*: 157)

Then he came to Eliot, Pound and Hulme, and the direction which Sisson was to follow as a reader, poet and critic. Sisson omits from this account the impact of the Latin classics and of French, German and Italian writing which from his early maturity marked him deeply. Among his first assured poems were translations of the German poet Heine, made during military service in the North-West Frontier Province during the Second World War. That time in Asia was his defining distance. When his troop-ship returned, through the Suez Canal into the Mediterranean, Sisson recognized with relief his own culture.

His poetry possesses a radicalism that has to do with roots, with the 'native tradition' as heard afresh after the ear has been 'retuned' by a formative experience – and by reading the work of a poet which actually alters him (in Sisson's case, it was Pound).

Thom Gunn 'quickly grew up after hearing someone suggest that Edith Sitwell was a bad poet'.

During the Blitz I was evacuated to a school in the country, where an enlightened English teacher taught from *The Poet's Tongue* (edited by W. H. Auden and John Garrett). . . . the anthology. . . emphasised the range and liveliness of poetry, by including mnemonics, popular songs, mummers' plays, nonsense poetry, songs by Blake, medieval fragments, and at one point two haunting lines from an Elegy of Donne's printed by themselves, as if they were a whole poem:

> Nurse oh My Love is slain, I saw him go
> Oer the white alps alone.

(*Worlds*: 58)

'And about this time', Gunn adds, 'I fell for Keats – fell for him as you do for the first poet who really means something to you. I read him all and liked him all, without discrimination. . . .' Reading *without discrimination* is an early step to becoming a good reader. It implies surrender, a surrender which begins in identification, but starts to weaken the mere subjectivity with which all reading begins.

Even the best readers, like poets, will eventually develop a closed pattern of taste. Having found what they like, they become increasingly sniffy about or indifferent to the rest. Readers – as T. S. Eliot noted ruefully to a friend – find it hard after the age of 40 to take new poets on board. A defensive conservatism, a hunger for the familiar, overcomes us, just as the young reader hungers for the new.

We need only look back at the reviews by critics of established distinction that greeted Ezra Pound and T. S. Eliot at the beginnings of their careers to see how 'modern poetry' can be resisted by the most literate and dedicated men of letters.

Arthur Waugh – a far from negligible editor and critic, father of Evelyn Waugh – wrote in *The Quarterly Review* in 1916 of Pound's 'wooden prose, cut into battens', of Eliot's 'premature decrepitude' in 'The Love Song of J. Alfred Prufrock', citing it as

> the reduction to absurdity of that school of literary license which, beginning with the declaration 'I knew my father well and he was a fool', naturally proceeds to the convenient assumption that everything which seemed wise and true to the father must inevitably be false and foolish to the son.

From Waugh's perspective Pound and Eliot produced 'unmetrical, incoherent banalities', and the hope for English poetry rested with the Georgians, against the 'drunken slave' at the feast, the Modern Poet. Waugh's hostility can stand for the many savage reviews that greeted the Modernists and helped them to the notoriety which made them – like all forbidden fruit – irresistible to a generation disaffected with the culture Waugh represented, and to its survival after the First World War.

It is hard nowadays for a poet to startle and rankle the Arthur Waughs: where Arthur Waughs exist, they tend to ignore rather than confront the challenge of the new, or to give it a welcome so as not 'to appear as fools in time's long glass'. Yet the energy of Waugh's criticism is worth a dozen temperate reviews which hedge their bets: it defines a cultural perspective honestly and emphatically, it resists what it sees as an affront, a perversion, and stimulates both the poets it assaults and the readership it addresses. In short, such criticism has a commitment to lived culture, a sense that poetry matters, and when we read it now it reflects upon its own age in a most useful fashion. At the same time it served to provoke a defining counterargument from Ezra Pound.

It was a catalyst which advanced the art of reading and, in an oblique way, the art of poetry. The advance was into tradition, not away from it. What was rejected was unreflecting conventionality. As the Polish poet Czeslaw Milosz has written, the protest against conventions, instead of taking us to some free space where a poet can encounter the world directly, as on the first day of Creation, again sends us back to those historical strata that already exist as form.

(Davie, *Czeslaw Milosz and the Insufficiency of the Lyric*: 23)

5

And yet if there was ever a *fox* in this undergrowth
it's long since vanished. There's only this one, this
   one here,
but we persevere because in a few minutes we can
all go for a drink. Then from nowhere
it occurs to me the fox's snout fits over its jaw
like the lid on a shoebox, and that's that.
I can relax. I push the note-pad aside like
a cleared dinner plate and slouch back in my chair.
If this is not a poem, I think, reading over my draft,
I'd like to know what is.

         Peter Sansom, 'The Fox in the Writing Class'

Today, tens of thousands of people write poems, but not many
write modern poetry. Among the hundreds of submissions that
reach my editorial desk each year, I discover minor contemporaries of Keats and Emily Brontë, Masefield and Edward
Thomas, or Christina Rossetti and Bishop Heber. Sometimes a
single assignation with Sylvia Plath or Robert Lowell seems to
jolt a writer into the 1960s. Many have a burning desire to be
published and an unshakeable belief in the sincerity and
originality of their work.

I suppose it's only natural that they should. Creative writing
courses are a catalyst. For a modest fee they provide two-finger
exercises in some version or other of the modern, critical
appraisal and encouragement. Yet the language, attitudes and
forms of such poetry are easily traceable. Like Sunday painters,
though rather more earnestly and with less delight, those
writers clutch at conventions and project within them a
language not naturally their own. They labour in a time-warp.

It is not the time-warp of apprenticeship. Blake wrote early
poems in imitation of Spenser as exercises in craft; the young
Thomas Hardy, too, translated Ecclesiastes into Spenserian

stanzas in order to master the form, and a subject-matter which he found powerfully congenial later in life. Keats learned in a similarly direct way from Spenser. Milton had learned from Spenser, too, and cast his own mighty spell on the poets who followed him. Each poet went back quite naturally to those 'historical strata that already exist as form', not in order to archaize but to find the present.

Spenser's stanza in *The Faerie Queene* is eight iambic pentameter lines and a final hexameter, with an ababbcbcc rhyme scheme. Simply by looking at the rhyme scheme one can detect multiple possibilities in such a form. There can be two couplet climaxes, for example, or the stanza can build to two different kinds of climax. The presence of an extra foot in the last line would seem to slow the progress of the poem stanza by stanza, giving an emphatic completeness to the ninth line with its couplet close; and yet the extra foot can push the rhythmic emphasis on to the opening of the next stanza. The variables the form offers the poet – for consecutive narrative, dialogue, argument, catalogue, description, and evocation – are infinite. Poets learning from Spenser master a form; they also master the presentation of every kind of content.

These stanzas from the fourth canto of the third book of *The Faerie Queene* (once allowance is made for their archaic orthography) have as great a poetic (if not a dramatic) immediacy as the blank verse lines of Shakespeare. That immediacy is a function of form and the selection and disposition of words that the form requires:

> Great Neptune stoode amazed at their sight,
> Whiles on his broad rownd back they softly slid,
> And eke him selfe mournd at their mournful plight,
> Yet wist not what their wailing ment; yet did,
> For great compassion of their sorrow, bid
> His mighty waters to them buxome bee:
> Eftesoones the roaring billowes still abid,
> And all the griesly Monsters of the See
> Stood gaping at their gate, and wondred them to see.

A teme of Dolphins raunged in aray
Drew the smooth charett of sad Cymoent:
They were all taught by Triton to obay
To the long raynes at her commaundement:
As swifte as swallowes on the waves they went,
That their brode flaggy finnes no fome did reare,
No bubling rowndell they behinde them sent.
The rest, of other fishes drawen weare,
Which with their finny oars the swelling sea did sheare.

When Hardy, Milton, and Blake did their Spenserian exercises to learn from the first great – perhaps the greatest – master of English prosody, they sought to develop skills in imitation: to understand how metre works in norm and variation; to control a stanza of the most complex and flexible kind; to counterpoint syntax and metre; and to select appropriate dictions. In Spenser they found epic, pastoral, and allegorical modes. All the figures of rhetoric were there. And Spenser opened out on wider traditions: earlier English poetry, Italy and the Renaissance, the Latin classics. Poets who imitated him did not give a bean for 'self-expression'. That hubris – so much a property of our own age – is fatal to the creation of works of art. It was corrected by imitation. Apprenticeship was a time when mere idiosyncrasies of language or thought (often the result of defective craftsmanship, wilfulness or ignorance) were purged.

The first skill of any writer is the skill to read. Before you can translate a line of Horace you must know Latin. Before you can write a Spenserian stanza you must understand its variable dynamic and potential. The Spenserian stanza is not an abstraction. It can be reduced to rules of metre and rhyme but the rules are almost accidental: mastering the form (as reader or writer) involves understanding why, not how it works. Coleridge understood Spenser's form, its place in the tradition and its exemplary importance when he described the Spenserian elements in his experience of Wordsworth's early poems:

It was not however the freedom from false taste, whether as to common defects, or to those more properly his own, which made so unusual an impression on my feelings immediately, and subsequently on my judgement. It was the union of deep feeling with profound thought; the fine balance of truth in observing with the imaginative faculty in modifying the objects observed; and above all the original gift of spreading the tone, the *atmosphere*, and with it the depth and height of the ideal world around forms, incidents, and situations, of which, for the common view, custom had bedimmed all lustre, and dried up the sparkle and the dew drops.

(*Biographia Literaria*: 48–9)

The Spenserian stanza is one example. We might just as well consider the sonnet, the heroic couplet, the ballad form. I take the Spenserian stanza because it has had so central a place in defining the English poetic tradition, yet Spenser has become one of the great unread poets of our time. A reader who is ignorant of Spenser or deaf to his work is likely to be deaf to crucial elements in the poetry of Milton, Wordsworth, and Keats, of Owen and Auden. Readers of modern poetry who neglect the determining poetry of the past impoverish their reading of the present. The early poems of Thom Gunn are muted if we are ignorant of Sidney, Greville, and Jonson; his later poems gain resonance for us if we know the work of Lawrence, Pound, and William Carlos Williams. Rhythmic patterns and the disposition of the lines on the page in the work of Charles Tomlinson may look highly original or simply quirky to the reader who has not encountered Williams; the intellectual elaboration of the earlier poems is elucidated by reading Wallace Stevens and Marianne Moore. It is not that Tomlinson *resembles* these three poets, but he has taken bearings from them, and it is helpful to be able to see what and how he has learned if we are to understand and assess his work. The marks that Edward Thomas has left on Andrew Motion, or that Patrick Kavanagh and Robert Lowell have left on Seamus Heaney, or that Ted Hughes has left on R. S. Thomas are eloquent in themselves, telling us something of the tenor of the poets influenced. The act of critical assessment is made more difficult, the emotional response is likely to be *merely* subjective, if the reader cannot – instinctively – make some of these connections for himself.

Poems – modern poems quite as much as those of the past – exist in relation to other poems from other times and languages, and much of their energy comes from that relationship. 'The Pentecost Castle' by Geoffrey Hill cannot quite be heard without at least a glimmering apprehension of Spanish ballads and the 'revenge' tradition in Spanish drama (with its parallels in Jacobean drama), without a feel for the English ballad tradition from which it departs and yet to which it seems to allude, without a memory of the Metaphysical poets, or without knowing Hill's own early poem 'Genesis', which it extends. The impact of these echoes, allusions, recollections, qualifications, is not academic, not critical, but imaginative. The poem works on the reader whether or not the parallels and contrasts are perceived, but the poem works for the reader, comes clear of individual subjectivity, the more the reader brings to it. Brings, not out of critical essays, reference books, and dictionaries, but out of active memory.

Active memory is to some extent involuntary, as involuntary as creative imagination can be. One of the most readerly of writers is Stevie Smith, even in her most arch and apparently awkward work. Many of her poems play off from a recollection of familiar cadences of Poe, Coleridge or Tennyson, and the poems are haunted by echoes. If those echoes are not heard, the poems can seem fey and inert. Some poets are possessed by a haunting echo and produce a poem with entirely inappropriate metre, like Philip Larkin's 'The Explosion', a moving poem until one begins to hear the metre of Longfellow's *Hiawatha*, or one of Betjeman's jollier pieces subverting the sombre subject, a mining disaster.

One of the noblest, exemplary readers in our literature is Coleridge. He wrote the best book I know about reading poetry. It does not set out to be a critical tome: it is a chronicle of his voyage of discovery through his own and earlier ages, and it is in his own age that he first finds his bearings. Sir Philip Sidney in his *Apology for Poetry* was a brilliant attorney for the defence, Dryden in his critical writings an urbane law-giver, and

Johnson the most eloquent of policemen who sometimes took the law into his own hands. But Coleridge, ballasted with tradition and philosophy, was a gentle, ill-organized adventurer who kept surprising himself, extending himself in new directions.

In his classic *Biographia Literaria* he writes,

> From causes which this is not the place to investigate, no models of past times, however perfect, can have the same vivid effect on the youthful mind as the productions of contemporary genius. (5)

As a young reader he was 'enthusiastically delighted and inspired' by the sonnets of William Lisle Bowles. Nowadays Bowles is read only by students of Coleridge, yet it would be wrong to suggest that Coleridge was injudicious in praising – and continuing to praise – him. Each writer – and reader – finds a personal way especially among contemporaries where no route-map has been drawn, and in an age like Coleridge's, the relative naturalness of Bowles's language looked bold, an orderly departure from the conventions that dominated poetry at the time. In assessing a writer's personal culture, what matters is less whom he admires than what form his admiration takes. Coleridge had mastered the classics. He knew his European and English traditions. He felt dissatisfaction with his own art and with the poetry of the period. In Bowles he had the first hint of what he was looking for, the first steps towards emancipation from tyrannous conventionality in form, theme, and language. Bowles was a faint foreshadowing of Wordsworth. Faint for us, but for Coleridge looking forward rather than back, the poems were clearly drawn.

6

I who am dead a thousand years
And wrote this crabbed post-classic screed
Transmit it to you – though with doubts
That you possess the skill to read,

Who, with your pink, mutated eyes,
Crouched in the radioactive swamp,
Beneath a leaking shelter, scan
These lines beside a flickering lamp,

Or in some plastic paradise
Of pointless gadgets, if you dwell,
And finding all your wants supplied
Do not suspect it may be Hell.

But does our art of words survive –
Do bards within that swamp rehearse
Tales of the twentieth century,
Nostalgic, in rude epic verse?. . .

John Heath-Stubbs, 'To a Poet a Thousand Years Hence'

Histories of poetry make the progress of the art look tidy. In the hands of professionals, periods and movements seem to define poets, rather than vice versa, and those writers who are unruly get left out or are treated as aberrant. There has always been critical unease about Smart, Cowper, and Goldsmith, Clare and Barnes, Clough, even about Blake, though they have always found advocates among articulate poets.

Some were perceived as eccentric or stigmatized as mad at the time that they were writing; they did not affect their age in the ways they might have done had their work been more widely read and understood. Instead, they remained curiosities. Once the train of tradition has set off, there is no provision for it to return and collect stragglers and oddballs.

Occasionally a rescue occurs, a long-dead writer is resurrected and found to be so astonishing, so fresh, that he exerts contemporary influence and makes it necessary for us to revise our sense of the past from which he has come. This happened with Emily Dickinson, for example, and with Gerard Manley Hopkins and, in a sense, with Edward Thomas, too. Charlotte Mew and Ivor Gurney have been more recent resurrections. Keith Douglas and, a few years ago, John Riley have found a place. It now seems unlikely that Wyndham Lewis will ever board the train except in the luggage of critics, and it sometimes seems doubtful in British eyes whether Ezra Pound will stay the journey.

On the other hand, some poets get frog-marched into movements with which they feel little affinity, and their work is presented in company they might not willingly have chosen. Thom Gunn has protested at being considered part of 'The Movement', and Elizabeth Jennings always looks out of place among the studied ironists, since hers is a poetry of deep vulnerability that refuses the social protection of a wry style. 'The Group' sometimes lays claim to Ted Hughes and Sylvia Plath. Members can insist that Plath and Hughes attended their meetings. It is hard to claim more than that.

Traditions themselves are not so categorical as the professional critics are in excluding or drafting writers, and there is an element of accident in what gets left behind. The accident may have to do with a poet's unfortunate choice of publisher. It may have to do with the company he keeps or with the quality of his critical advocates. Some insist that, in the past, it has been a function of gender, class, or race, and that these exclusions continue. It can be a matter of politics. It is most likely to be a problem of diction or formal choices.

The poems of Elizabeth Daryush, for instance, are written in a language that looks old-fashioned, not to say archaic. She remains an engaging writer, a philosophical poet of great rigour. Coming to her work with distrust born of a diet of irony, we read the 'thees' and 'thous', the odd inversions and abstract words, with condescension. We might even be tempted to condescend to her last-published and most ambitious poem,

'Air and Variations', with its formal tribute to her father Robert
Bridges' friend Gerard Manley Hopkins in the form and movement – as in the eighth stanza:

> I said: I have seen
> The wall of a mountainous wave
> Foam into spheres, then sink through green
> Of fields to a human grave;
> I have followed a sky-filled river, whose flickering
> throe
> Leapt from its actual nodes, to a moon-tide gave
> Its might . . . nor forward urge nor backward
> formed that flow,
> Each was the older twin . . .

She will never be read except by a few – poets, and scholars
curious about the woman who, in the same year as Marianne
Moore, 'invented' syllabic verse. Yet here and in many of her
terse short poems there is a formal and intellectual mastery,
and in the rhythms an ascetic passion for ideas and images that
quicken her pulse. There is little chance of her work appealing
to feminist critics though it raises in the purest form some of the
arguments of language and gender, formal tradition and
gender, which should be addressed.

Wyndham Lewis was condemned to the 'impalpable dark
prison of neglect' because of his politics. His satire *One Way
Song* deserves an audience. The 'Envoi' which concludes the
poem remains a forthright *ars poetica*:

> If I have not trod the romantic path, blame me!
> If it has been a man singing and not a bird –
> If so the bird you be to curse, curse me
> Poor Parrot! Then I will teach you *another* word!
> If plain speech brings the blush beneath the dirt
> I'm sorry if you hate the thing you heard –
> But I meant that you should get it, classic and clear,
> Between the eyes, or in the centre of the ear!
> As plain as the 'Burgess-gentleman' got his
> In natural verses, or the 'Ridiculous Miss',

These times require a tongue that naked goes,
Without more fuss than Dryden's or Defoe's.

The echo of Skelton's most witty, demotic and chaotic poem 'Speak Parrot' in the fourth line suggest a hit-or-miss approach, and Lewis's poem wavers between savage precision and demonic possession, between straight-talk and rant. Dryden stands here for a writer with an essentially social or public style capable of tackling any subject, while Defoe is the paradigm for a prose style utterly unselfconscious and down-to-earth. Published in 1933, *One Way Song* is a polemic aimed very directly at an age whose fashions – literary and political – Lewis found increasingly uncongenial. It belongs perhaps too narrowly to its time and its occasions. It did not exactly misfire, but the targets it aimed at were insubstantial: the satirical arrow flew through them and fell from view.

Roy Campbell has fallen (only temporarily, I trust) from view for the same reasons as Lewis – his political complexion. He has also been victim of the prejudice against long poems (and against an impure, digested modernism, too) which made the emergence of David Jones as a major writer seem more a conspiracy of critics than an act of literary restitution. Will anyone ever take the long works of George Barker, John Heath-Stubbs, and W. S. Graham in the terms that they propose? Will Henry Reed ever be more than a single anthology piece and a brilliant parody? Why has Vernon Watkins been neglected? Will Andrew Young, E. J. Scovell, Cliff Ashby, Burns Singer, Daniel Huws, and Thomas Blackburn find more than a precarious survival? Can we have a purchase on modern poetry without knowing their work? It has much to give – much that is not to be found elsewhere on the poetry shelves.

The failure to accommodate awkward, challenging poems is not a strictly contemporary phenomenon. John Skelton's work and the *Elegies* of Christopher Marlowe are 'aberrant'. Yet aberration, anachronism, even apparent madness, have energies, especially – as I have suggested – when the dominant conventions of poetry become rigid in the diction, tones, or themes deemed admissible by the legislators of taste. The history of

54

English poetry is not lapidary: it can be revised. The enthusiasm of Swinburne, and later Eliot, for John Donne, led to revaluation of a neglected area of English poetry, just as Wesley and Coleridge helped to re-establish the reputation of George Herbert (though Wesley squeezed some of Herbert's poems a little brutally to fit them on the Procrustean bed of his hymn stanzas). But the re-emergence of the Metaphysicals has entailed the neglect of the Cavaliers and Sons of Ben. How much longer will it be considered heresy to speak of Herrick in the same breath with Donne?

And the extraordinarily high value placed on the poems of Thomas Hardy since the 1930s can be explained only in the light of the creative strategies of the poets who have championed his work, for whom he can sometimes seem a talisman against the encroachments of 'the new'.

Every age draws the route-map to the city where it thinks it lives. Spenser has been virtually abandoned on the contemporary map; Milton is no longer an acknowledged junction. Cowper and Clare and Smart begin to be valued properly, but generally at the expense of their contemporaries.

Each poet draws a map, too, and establishes a kind of legitimacy in relation, not only to conventions of the time, but to traditions which inform a distinctive (though not necessarily a personal) idiom. The reader who wants to understand the dynamic of the poems of Ted Hughes will want to read Shakespeare, the Jacobeans, D. H. Lawrence, the poets of Eastern Europe whose work Hughes has advocated in Britain, and other poets such as Emily Dickinson and Keith Douglas, whose work he has fed upon, remote though the affinities may seem. Reading is an act of memory as well as an act of construction. Not to sense an echo of Emily Dickinson and a counter-echo of Hopkins in the opening line of Ted Hughes's 'Thrushes' is to miss a dimension of the poem. It is not only an indication of what Hughes has taken to heart from his predecessors but of how he has taken it to heart, how from Emily Dickinson he has absorbed the energy rather than the precision of her peculiar diction and subtly conventional rhythms, how from Hopkins he has drawn mimetic rather than philosophical elements.

Reading modern poetry is not a scholarly but a cultural act: to find connections. The poem is free-standing, perhaps; but even so it is not a denial of context. It inevitably proposes relations, it stands within the language and has rhythmic, etymological and semantic roots. Or, altering the metaphor, tradition is a subtle echo-chamber in which the reader grows sensitive to resonances. Delight in the miracles of certain enjambements, certain strokes of diction, or a formal satisfaction in a cadence or a whole poem: such pleasures are not trivial. They are the energizing force of poetry, the precisions which set the art of poetry apart from other verbal arts. The reader who regards such pleasures as peripheral to questions of 'meaning' is more likely to be a critic with a system than a natural reader of poetry. The abiding meaning of any poem is a function of technical properties – whether deliberately or accidentally achieved – which give it life beyond its occasion and its 'ideas'.

Rhythm, diction, structure, and form become more urgent concerns for the responsive reader than a poet's informing mythologies or ideas, propriety of sentiment, 'sincerity', or thematic relevance. The best poets are aware of this paradox: that the language of poetry is a language of truth only if it is truthful in conception and in the connections between the technical endeavour and the emotional occasion. It does not assert, it enacts. Donald Davie's poem 'July 1964' addresses the issue with punishing candour (*Collected Poems*, 1972).

> I smell a smell of death.
> Roethke, who died last year
> with whom I drank in London,
> wrote the book I am reading;
> a friend, of a firm mind,
> has died or is dying now,
> a telegram informs me;
> the wife of a neighbour died
> in three quick months of cancer.
>
> Love and art I practise;
> they seem to be worth no more
> and no less than they were.

The firm mind practised neither.
It practised charity
vocationally and
yet for the most part truly.
Roethke, who practised both,
was slack in his art by the end.

The practice of an art
is to convert all terms
into the terms of art.
By the end of the third stanza
death is a smell no longer;
it is a problem of style.
A man who ought to know me
wrote in a review
my emotional life was meagre.

But the reader does not look coldly for solutions to 'problems of style', the technical excellences which produce the kinds of local epiphany that – by his own report – made Housman's hair stand on end. The experienced reader is attuned to respond to them. One can grow attuned only through reading and reading deeply, learning poems and passages by heart. Reading criticism, studying literary programmes or books of prosody can be pleasurable and helpful to a degree, but cannot displace the encounter with the poem. When poetry is taught in schools and in further education, the reader's pulse and its relationship with the pulse of the poem tend to get neglected in discussions of theme and poetic intention, and yet there is more poetry in Blake's poems, or Yeats's, or Shelley's, in Milton's, or Herbert's, or Hopkins's, than in their ideas, and the poems are sometimes better than the poet's intentions for them. Some poems rise out of the most solemn twaddle, and yet they move us more deeply than we care to admit. Shelley's 'Adonais', for example, or Blake's 'The Book of Thel', have what Conrad Aiken once called 'residual magic' that has little to do with their ideas and everything to do with technical properties, achieved tone, through-rhythm, which make a sense far deeper than the dubious informing ideas.

How does this instinctive hearing work in the echo-chamber of tradition? As a resource of memory and imagination, the tradition does not exist chronologically, any more than our reading of poetry follows a chronological sequence from Chaucer to Hill. I came to love Eliot's 'Ash Wednesday' when I was at school. As an undergraduate I chanced upon the poem by Guido Cavalcanti which informs the opening lines of Eliot's poem. The elation of familiarity was great – as though Cavalcanti had quoted favourite lines of Eliot in Italian. The poetry of the present can make the past familiar – thus Donald Davie's poems help us to read Goldsmith and Cowper as well as Pasternak and Pound; the poems of C. H. Sisson help us read Swift and Vaughan as well as Eliot and Lewis. There is always reciprocity between poetries. I emphasize 'always': readers who confine themselves to contemporary poetry and are impatient of the remoteness of Ralegh, Chapman's Homer, Herrick, Rochester, Smart, or Clough, deny themselves dimensions of pleasure and understanding *in the present*. Traditions are erratic continuums; but every poem has a history not only in the poet's imagination and the poem's occasion, but in an informing past.

And your dialect blurred with locality, I think,
As the grapes with mist. We work along the rows
Stripping the bunches from the vines, while I puzzle
For sense in this tender meaningless conceit.

> Robert Wells, 'Vendemmia'

W. H. Auden wrote a kind of creed in the introduction to the
The Poet's Tongue – the influential anthology he prepared in
1935 with John Garrett. What he says is not novel: it can be
traced to Wordsworth, or further back (with a little distortion)
to Sidney, or even to Dante. But he says it with the emphasis
and authority of a scout master. It is still taken to heart by
many English critics, teachers, and readers. I think it is false,
or at best a half-truth, and limiting in the way Auden proposes
it.

He declares: 'Of the many definitions of poetry, the simplest
is still the best: "memorable speech".' We surrender to the
poem 'as we do when talking to an intimate friend'. The statement is qualified, rather in the way that Wordsworth in his
'Preface' to *Lyrical Ballads* qualifies his notion of diction. But
like Wordsworth's manifesto, Auden's is unbalanced by its
categorical nature. Other poets who share Auden's view have
been more circumspect. Donald Davie insists that poetry is
'considered speech', a phrase rather more precise and inclusive
than 'memorable speech', and a host of poets and critics share
the view in their prose utterances, though their work time after
time seems to contradict it.

Auden valued the poems of Thomas Hardy for very different
reasons from those adduced by John Crowe Ransom, the
American poet and critic. Auden admires *authority* in poets, and
in Hardy he finds a poet who speaks, and speaks from a great
height, whose perspectives and ironies he admires. Ransom, in
turn, valuing other poems than those Auden would single out

in the vast body of Hardy's work, loves the poet who understood 'the three dimensions of a poem': plot, metres, and
poetic language, 'the flowering habit of a thing that is alive,
displaying its grace generally and coming into intermittent
focus in special configurations of leaf or blossom.' The phrase
'intermittent focus' is so apposite to Hardy's work because it
acknowledges, behind the 'memorable speech' of the poems, a
necessity within the poet to bring things difficult to define into
focus – a creative, not a social pressure – and the 'intermittence'
of its success. It reminds us of Hardy's roots in the nineteenth
century and sets him back a little from where contemporary
critics like to place him, square on the threshold, trying to bolt
the door of English poetry against Modernism.

Thomas Hardy is not what has been made of him in the last
quarter-century in Britain, a prophylactic against Anglo-
American Modernism and free verse, a poet for whom 'craft'
had meaning and who made modest claims for his work (those
who admire his modesty fail to note the hint of irony in it). It
is not that Hardy has been over-valued, it seems to me; but in
an age of 'corrupt eloquence' he has been misvalued. He has
more in common with Pound (who admired his poems) than
with some of those who use his work more often than they read
it. Donald Davie in his excellent, contentious book *Thomas
Hardy and British Poetry* called Hardy 'the most far-reaching
influence, for good or ill . . . in British poetry of the last fifty
years'. He describes the limitations of Hardy's art in terms I
find plausible indeed:

> it begins to look as if Hardy's engaging modesty and his
> decent liberalism represent a crucial selling short of the poetic
> vocation, for himself and his successors. For surely the poet,
> if anyone, has a duty to be radical, to go to the roots. So
> much at least all poets have assumed through the centuries.
> Hardy, perhaps without knowing it, questions that assump-
> tion, and appears to reject it. Some of his successors in
> England, and a few out of England, seem to have agreed with
> him.   (110)

Davie describes Hardy's *effect* in his successors: 'Hardy has the effect of locking any poet he influences into a world of historical contingency, a world of specific places at specific times.' Is it a matter of direct influence or is Hardy merely the earliest and most copious witness to a condition that has become endemic to a modern British imagination emancipated from faith and seeking solace in history, landscape, and local incident? Certainly the triumph of 'historical contingency' sometimes looks pretty complete. It may be that in these historical and cultural circumstances, a social, spoken mode comes to dominate literary work.

Poetry can have much to do with speech. Yet even at its most idiomatic it is different in construction both in its rhythmic patterning (however naturally that patterning grows out of speech cadences) and in its semantic intention. The Comte de Buffon wrote, in an age when the language of literature and the language of polite society were alike highly formalized: 'Those who write as they speak, even though they speak well, write badly.' Even within the work of Wordsworth, the most deliberately 'spoken' poems and passages are not invariably memorable. When Dorothy is imagined within earshot, the poet does much more than speak. Auden's 'intimate friend', the hypothetical interlocutor, is not a necessary reality for Wordsworth.

I rather doubt that he was a reality for a poet so narcissistic even in his politics as the young Auden was, either, any more than Yeats's idealized fisherman was really likely to be enthusiastic about 'Hic et Ille' or to recognize a poem cold and passionate as the dawn. The language of intimate friendship – 'overheard rather than heard' though it may be – is peculiar to that intimacy, a shorthand which does not require – which indeed rejects – exposition and which hedges out the common world by code, not by irony. Against such notions one can propose Coleridge's definitions: 'a more than usual state of emotion, with more than usual order'; 'balance or reconciliation of opposite or discordant qualities'; or the line he quotes which – abstracting though it is – has an eloquence like Wordsworth's 'stationary blasts of waterfalls': 'Making a quiet image of disquiet'. Poems are undeniably made out of the same elements as speech or prose in terms of dictions, syntax and rhythms. The difference is in the ways those elements are combined and in the impulses which effect their combination.

If love of poetry for reader and writer begins early with nursery rhymes, ballads and song, the difference from speech is patent at the outset. The attraction to poetry is an attraction to something notably different from prose or speech. Indeed, the historical origins of poetry were in ceremonial, ritualized language, whether the patterned sounds of the words related to the gods in prayer or liturgy, to heroic legend or to repetitive labour. If as a modern poet matures his poems develop towards speech patterns, they do not aspire to equivalence with speech.

One of the most apparently spoken or speaking poets of our time is John Ashbery. One need only hear his public readings to appreciate how the voice of his poems is continuous with his speaking voice. Or is it? The word 'voice' will not do. Ashbery has voices, modulations different in tone and mood, relating differently to elements in past poetry, in present experience, and in various areas of cultural and social allusion. It is a matter of registers of speech and reference which are discriminated, harmonized, mingled, merged. His is a poetry which takes strands of language and the emotions, ideas and histories which pertain to them or emerge from the contrasts between them. Experience is conveyed by voices, not a voice; the poet is an orchestrator, not a speaker in a lyrical first-person way. This does not make the poems less personal, but it does remove the personal element from the area of 'personality'. A poetry which develops out of an attuned sense of the diversified languages of our tradition and the diverse social language of our time can be read as 'memorable speech' of course, but it does not necessarily imply a speaker or a specific 'intimate' interlocutor.

Donald Davie, writing about Czeslaw Milosz, contrasts his approach with C. H. Sisson's.

Within the conventions that govern poetic utterance, still operative in our day though seldom stated, Sisson's use of language was thoroughly responsible and honest. What I seemed to have discovered in Milosz was a poet who found no use for one set of such conventions, those that govern the meditative lyric. In such poems – Gray's 'Elegy' is one of them surely, and Wordsworth's 'Tintern Abbey' is another – the poet occupies a fixed point in a landscape, and the assertions that he makes are to be understood as true only in relation to that fixed point, in the context of a special occasion and a mood which that occasion provokes. Sisson's 'In the West Country' observed those conventions; no poem in *Bells in Winter* observed them, for the good reason (as I now noticed) that the speaker of those poems occupied no fixed point for the duration of his poem but on the contrary was always flitting, moving about. And what I saw was what had baffled, had almost literally disoriented and therefore irritated me.

(*Czeslaw Milosz and the Insufficiency of the Lyric*: 4–5)

Davie's argument goes to the heart of what some of the best modern poetry seems to attempt with language. For the 'flitting' poet's wings are his language, and the movement away from single focused experience is also a movement away from consistently constructed language, from refined dictions and continuous registers. Indeed, the freedom is manifest in Milosz as, very differently, in Ashbery, and differently again – though Davie might not agree with this – in poems by Sisson such as 'In Insula Avalonia'. Here we witness it in alterations of poetic perspective, the 'language of disorientation' which has been attributed variously to Allen Tate, David Jones, and Geoffrey Hill – work in which semantic nuance is deliberately disturbed and short-circuited so that context redefines words very precisely. It is also evident in the choice of registers and dialects with which the poet makes his poem. It may be by variations in diction, in or out of metrical regularity, it may be by specific allusion to a poem or a convention of the past, whether ironically or elegiacally called up.

All the resources of what Davie, adopting an image of André Malraux's, calls 'the imaginary museum' – all the literature of the past and present – are there for the poet to draw on, and the poet draws knowingly as well as instinctively. Poetry can no longer – if it ever could – be usefully considered as a continuation of speech in formal terms. We can say this without going as far as the critic Roman Jacobson who calls poetry 'organized violence committed against common speech'. Yet the more the language of the poem resembles speech, the more likely the modern poet's manner is to be ironic, and speech itself to have parodic intent as in Clough's *Amours de Voyage* or Browning's monologues or Auden's domestic poems. Speech constructed for a *persona* is speech at one remove from the poet and at two removes from the 'intimate friend'. Some memorable poetry of the past and some challenging poetry of our own time stays in mind precisely because it is remote from speech – remote in that it resembles song, or liturgical usage, because it has a contrived consistency as in dramatic writing, or because it has visual properties crucial to its structure which only the eye can 'hear'. Remote because it insists on its difference of construction from everyday spoken language.

8

You cannot start a poem without a word.
  Speak none, for then the silence is absurd.
Even the fishes swim against the tide.
  And do you never want to be outside?
Great God, your prisoner weeps, and so do I.
  Miracles are arranged accordingly.
Ite, ite but you shall not go forth.
  Is it not prison for two pennyworth?
Sleep behind walls. There shall be sleep
  Revelatory as it shall be deep.
Two sides, two pillows. Truth lays its head on one.
  Is there another or shall love have none?
The body, yes. How shall it walk this way?
  Shall it be indiscriminate and pray?
Is love then over all? Are these trees
  Also cared for, oratory breeze?
They are of the flesh of the cross,
  Lignum, the wood he hung on; what he was,
Corpus & sanguis not to be saved alive.
  That so, would it not better be
To be metamorphosed Daphne?

                         C. H. Sisson, 'Daphne'

In the foreword to *In the Trojan Ditch,* his collected poems and
selected translations (1974), C. H. Sisson wrote:

> There is no question, as it has come to me, of filling note-
> books with what one knows already. Indeed as the inevitable
> facility comes, the conscious task becomes the rejection of
> whatever appears with the face of familiarity. The writing of
> poetry is, in a sense, the opposite of writing what one wants
> to write, and it is because of the embarrassing growth of the
> area of consciousness which writing, as indeed the other

serious encounters of life, produces that one has recourse to the conscious manipulation of translation, as it were to distract one while the unwanted impulses free themselves under the provocation of another's thought.

(The Avoidance of Literature: 462)

This personal statement is, on the face of it, eccentric. It refers not so much to subject-matter and theme as to the technical properties of the poem, and particularly to its rhythmical character. Eccentric, and yet it has come back to me as I read poems by other writers which take root in my memory. The difficult and faulted sequence 'Sonnets for a Dying Man' by Burns Singer, or his astonishing 'narrative' called 'The Transparent Prisoner'; *Villa Stellar* and *Anno Domini* by George Barker; 'Johann Joachim Quantz's Five Lessons' and 'To My Wife at Midnight' by W. S. Graham; Donald Davie's vulnerable and hectic poem *In the Stopping Train*; Geoffrey Hill's 'Pentecost Castle' sequence; James Fenton's 'A German Requiem': these are among the works, some by poets noted for their austerity and control, others by the more lavish temperaments bred up in the 1940s, which have a quality of being written in a different way, out of a different source, from the poems which make up the bulk of readable verse in our time.

Despite – or because of – their technical complexity, which amounts to virtuosity in some cases, their idiosyncrasy and personality (for each of these poems is in some ways the most *personal* writing of which the poet has been capable) were secondary to the impulse of the poem, which was 'impersonal' to the extent that the creative processes themselves – memory and imagination – seemed to become the subject of the poem.

It is not a question of afflatus or inspiration, I think. Rather, the poems are the result of a pressure of complex and not entirely apprehended (or controlled) content. The poet 'has something to say', but that 'something' is not a statement detachable from the act of saying. It is implicit to an unusual degree in the very form and process of articulation. Of course no poem can be fully paraphrased, but many – perhaps most – of the poems we read offer a 'meaning', a point of climax that

releases the burden of the poem, that makes it possible for
reader, teacher, or critic to get hold of it and talk about it from
the outside in, from 'what the poem says' to 'how it says'. The
poems that are genuinely 'the opposite of writing what one
wants to write' cannot be readily approached in this way.

Describing C. H. Sisson's 'In Insula Avalonia' when it first
appeared in book form, Donald Davie spoke of the interweav-
ing of themes 'in a verse which, as it were, goes nowhere and
says nothing, which is Shakespearean and Eliotic to just the
degree that it is Virgilian'. Davie's statement, which at first
seems obscure, is wonderfully precise. The poem can be
approached only on its own terms. The terms are given in the
language and the poetic processes, and cannot be extrapolated.
It was on the strength of this, one of Sisson's finest poems, that
his publisher invited him to translate Dante's *Divine Comedy*
and later Virgil's *Aeneid*. The poem's language brings into play
the chief elements of which Sisson's imagination is woven, just
as in Dante's great poem Virgil is at no point absent. Imagination is haunted by its antecedents, its 'influences', though
'influence' is altogether too feeble to describe the constitutive
nature in Dante's mind of Virgil, or in Sisson's mind of Dante.

In the third section of the poem, for example, the three line
stanzas call up *terza rima* without submitting to Dante's rhyme
scheme, and the ways in which the observed world is trans-
figured by metaphor relate to Dante's transformations, as to
Ovid's. The presence of Virgil, of the English pastoral tradition,
and the Arthurian tradition merge, too, in a pagan-Christian
language without parallel among Sisson's contemporaries
because the poetry, for all its allusiveness, is rooted at once in
an actual landscape, in real particulars, and in history and an
historical faith. The two swans on the darkening river transform
it into a serpent. The poem is 'literal' even in the emotional
(and historical) metamorphoses of the given world. The wealth
of language and imagination brings into focus not a world teem-
ing with promise but a seasonal and personal desolation:

> Dark wind, dark wind that makes the river black
> Two swans upon it are the serpent's eyes –

Wind through the meadows as you twist your heart.

Twisted are trees, especially this oak
Which stands with all its leaves throughout the year;
There is no Autumn for its golden boughs

But winter always and the lowering sky
That hangs its blanket lower than the earth
Which we are under in this Advent-tide.

Not even ghosts. The banks are desolate
With shallow snow between the matted grass
Home of the dead but there is no one here.

This is a language of enactment, given to Sisson at least in part because, for him, the Incarnation was not a metaphor when he wrote the poem, and the fact of Advent more than a page on the calendar.

The kinds of poem I have been trying to describe probably perplex the poet who recognizes himself in them, but a self that has eluded the control of the 'conscious' artist. There is a poet behind the deliberate, manipulative post-modern writer, a poet of an older kind. If poetry is 'responsible speech', there are at least two kinds of responsibility, the more common kind a practice of control, the less common a practice of submission.

The ability to submit to the urgent pressure of content, to let the unfamiliar find expression, is given to a few writers and then only in their maturity. I am persuaded that in our time as in the past these are the best writers in the sense that, against the grain of fashion and even of their own inclination, they take the language of poetry further, deeper if you like, than their contemporaries have done. They extend the art, as if by accident. There is a gulf between this kind of writing and the deliberate and deliberated confessionalism of poets who have learned from Robert Lowell, or those who abandon traditional forms and attempt to engage what they have called the 'deep image'. And there is a poetry which – to borrow Robert Nye's phrase about Dylan Thomas – confuses 'depth' with 'thickness', an observation we might wish to apply to the work of Peter Redgrove or Jeremy Reed. Here there is a pressure of language, not of content, and in such circumstances the poet is not the means, but the end.

The genuine article has little to do with myth-making, confession, or exorcism. It has to do with re-establishing continuities, with chancing upon that wholeness of vision which Edgell Rickword, in the passage already quoted, attributes to Donne at his noblest. Poets are only rarely at their noblest.

The kind of poetry I have been trying to describe is probably the hardest to assess when it is close to us in time. Burns Singer wrote in 'The Gentle Engineer':

> It is my own blood nips at every pore
> And I myself the calcified treadmark of
> Process towards me:
> All of a million delicate engines whisper
> Warm now, to go now
> Through dragnets of tunnels forwards as my life.
> I carry that which I am carried by.

The last line has a staying resonance. In what comes before, the reader may feel ill at ease. There is what at first appears the loose gesture of 'All of a million', yet it is not Yeats's catchall 'all', and 'a million' (in context) is not a vague cop-out: it seems to have a specific function beyond the rhetorical. In the genitive constructions there is the 1940s twitch one associates with Dylan Thomas, Nicholas Moore, and the early W. S. Graham, and yet the syntax here, and the enjambements, are enactive: the poem is feeling its way among meanings, and the reversals in metre break what would be a rhetorical flow into a phrased and tentative progression.

9

We have to love the past
it is our invention. Perhaps, after all
forgiveness is the proper attitude
and we should not abolish history but make a space
    in it
of eighteenth-century boudoirs and the Kingdom of
    Meroe,
the Empire of Songhoi . . .

                  John Ash, 'The Rain'

Tradition may not be a simple continuum, and yet it embodies a kind of progression. It is possible to allude to things in it, to take things from it, but to go back is not allowed. Some of the poems of C. H. Sisson give the sense of rhyme without rhyming: it is a function of rhythm more than metaphorical structure which relates the strict, complex stanza form of 'Money', 'The Person' and the rebarbative long poem 'The Discarnation' to the work of the Metaphysicals. Other pieces adopt heroic couplets but use them in a broken, awkward way, so the form recalls a no longer available resource, the closed couplet with its authoritative completeness, and the age of common values that sustained it. Others still are balladic, or touch upon nursery rhyme, but always with elements which are deliberately jarring, which will not be assimilated.

These formal allusions, what one critic calls 'the approximate Muse', are deeply affecting – elegiac in quality if one detects them and feels the distance of those proposed models which yet possess a referential centrality. Without this recognition, the couplets can look merely rough-hewn and awkward; the unrhymed tetrameters which seem to rhyme can have an untraceable resonance. To say that the couplets are awkward, that the tetrameters have a puzzling magic, is correct, but falls short of their formal significance. Such 'approximations' can be found in the poems of Geoffrey Hill, W. S. Graham, Stevie Smith, Ted Hughes, Philip Larkin, and Donald Davie. They are present in the work of the great Modernists, in Pound's *Mauberley* and 'Propertius' as well as the *Cantos*, in Eliot's 'Dry Salvages' and elsewhere in his verse and prose. When I say they are affective 'if one detects them' I should perhaps say 'if they detect us': the formal allusion distinguishes us, singles us out at the point of recognition and brings us into the process of the poem.

Poets can imitate without allusion: it is important to distinguish a difference of effect here. It is the difference between achieved poetry and mere pastiche. In his weak poems Vaughan imitates Herbert. In their plays Wordsworth and later Shelley imitate Shakespeare. In such cases the later poet is trying to achieve the authority of an earlier or greater model and in so doing displaces the dynamics of his own language, his own formal imagination. In such imitations there is a failure of perspective, of the necessary irony that validates the later poem as allusive rather than imitative.

Aspiring poets who write now as though Eliot and Pound never lived and long for – say – a Keatsian lushness, a Georgian composure and an untrammelled relationship between language and the things it names, generally imitate not the dynamic of Keats's sonnets and stanza forms but the effects of his diction, the surface of his rhetoric. That rhetoric is grounded in technical competences and in correspondences between the poet's natural language and his experience of the world that cannot be reproduced. It belongs so intimately to his imaginative reality that his poems, even the earliest and the most lavish, retain a force for which we need make no allowances today, even after Modernism has taught us to distrust abstraction and apparently naked emotion. Keats is more our contemporary than even his finest imitators. Being of his time, he is of ours as well, much as Marlowe, Dryden, and Cowper are. He is our contemporary more than Wilfred Owen, who learned so much from him, and in spite of Owen's perennial thematic appeal.

Being modern has to do not with whom the poet imitates or

rejects (functions of judgement, of training) but with the appositeness of his language (diction and rhythm) to the chosen themes, and the confidence with which that language engages those themes. Antique diction has a place in certain poems; traditional forms are not redundant; and yet there is a necessary place for the formal legacies of Modernism.

To identify the second-hand, that is an essential skill for the reader of modern poetry. But modern poetry cannot be positively characterized. There is no main stream, no dominant mode. At a time when critical ideologies are in conflict and various 'schools' of poetry thrive, there are poets and critics, influential reviewers and anthologists, who disparage whole areas of resource and achievement. Yvor Winters and F. R. Leavis, and latterly Helen Vendler and Kingsley Amis, for example, turn their backs (very lucidly) on much that strikes the mere reader as wonderful. An acquired orthodoxy can enable writers and students to find their way among the undergrowth of recent and past literature, to dismiss centuries as irrelevant and void, to scrub whole cities of contemporary writers from the map. But orthodoxy does not help readers very much.

It is unlikely that the reader developing a taste for poetry will seek to give it theoretical coherence. Generalization – for the reader – spells impoverishment. Those who write off the eighteenth century, for example, close themselves in a very narrow place. Apart from anything else, the nineteenth century makes very little sense without the eighteenth. And the curious reader makes discoveries: Marlowe's translations of Ovid suddenly strike him as miraculous: is it possible that they may be more suggestive to us today in terms of form and tone than Donne's poems are? Might Gower not emerge a little further from the shadow of Chaucer when a reader discovers that Amans, embedded though he is in the *Confessio Amantis*, is one of the great love poets in the language? He may find himself gazing into the classics through new English translations and identifying there – in a Virgil, or a Heine – some of the best contemporary poetry, energetic and achieved, the most lived.

Odd that translation should be so enabling – yet throughout our literary history it has been so. Chaucer and Wyatt,

Shakespeare and Dryden, Shelley and Pound, have made distinctive marks in their Englishing of foreign and classic poetry, whether assimilating it into their own work or billing it as 'translation'. One could write a history of English poetry – the changing attitudes to form, metre, diction, and subject-matter – simply by comparing translations down the centuries of Virgil, or of Horace's *Satires* and *Odes* (and noting when, and why, poets turned their attention from the *Satires* to the *Odes*).

Interest in poetry in translation today is rather different from interest before the First World War. When poets took bearings from Virgil or Dante, or translated Ronsard, Petrarch, Calderón or Goethe, they were drawing on what was perceived as a catholic European tradition, rooted in the Classics. It was hard not to see things in this way, right up to the end of the eighteenth century. Chaucer and Boccaccio, Camoẽs and Tasso, Sidney and Petrarch – alien though they were in temperament, and despite the distances between their languages, their work seemed to be part of a common cultural enterprise. The enriching exchange between vernacular literatures rooted in Latin and Greek and in the Bible was a given: there was a coherence which made radical departures the more eloquent. An enabling continuity between cultures persisted into this century, though educational developments and political change, with the emergence of increasingly insistent nationalisms, eroded common elements between French and English, German and English, much more rapidly and decisively than the religious and dynastic conflicts of earlier centuries had done.

Today some poets still converse with that European tradition and draw confidently on Virgil and Dante, Goethe and Lope de Vega, Racine and Pushkin, just as Pushkin drew on Byron, and Pound on the Provençal poets. But there is another approach to translation especially of contemporary work – which sees it as a means of emancipation from a native tradition and seizes upon 'primitive' or new poetries to justify theories such as the 'deep image'. Or poets look to the achievements of Eastern European writers and see them as endowed by turbulent history with greater seriousness in their break with their own

74

literary past than the English poet can hope to achieve except through imitation.

The Yugoslav poet Vasko Popa illustrates the peril of such an approach for English poets. Quite apart from the difference in dynamic between his language and ours, and the fact that our best access to his work is through translations which possess little semantic resonance, bringing into English only his disrupted imagery and dismembered narrative, there is the fact that his poetry relates to a popular, not a classical, tradition, is rooted in the equivalent to a folk or balladic tradition quite allien to our own. We receive him in English as something of a Modernist, though in some respects he represents the perennial flowering of a kind of popular poetry for which we have no living English equivalent. He is, in short, mis-received, and though his procedures are full of hints and shadows, it is not his poems but what they are believed to represent that attracts the English writer. And the English reader? Peter Porter in an interview a decade and a half ago commented on the feverish interest in translation: 'What worries me about translation is quite simply this: that it is burdened with so much good will. And good will is what gets in the way of anything being properly realised.' In translation of contemporary poetry, the intention can be more generous than the deed.

There is a rich tradition of mis-reading in English poetry. Hart Crane's enthusiastic embrace of French Surrealism, or Dylan Thomas's less fruitful approach to the same phenomenon, have been important. But mis-reading (which when poets do it we might prefer to call 'imaginative reading') involves reading, a familiarity with original texts, a sense (in the case of the French Surrealists) that their work was creating a deliberate discontinuity within a tradition which was lived and understood, so that the discontinuity itself had coherence only in relation to what it set itself against. The success of the Surrealist project – which was so manifestly of its own time – is reversed by the way in which it has in turn become canonical.

Mis-reading is one thing, while the selection of poets not for what they write but for what they represent is something quite different. The Polish writers Czeslaw Milosz and Zbigniew

Herbert bring much with them into English because they are part of the beleaguered catholic European tradition. Their allusions, ironies, formal choices, have parallels or equivalents in English. Indeed, they have drawn on English models themselves. Their work, apart from its vivid texture, has been well translated. But Popa, or Miroslav Holub, are different in kind. Their relationship with their own culture, their rootedness in the semantics of their vernaculars and their popular traditions (whether balladic or journalistic), means that it is impossible to *read* them in English. They exist for us as talismans. Their work is not exemplary, but their presence is. Poets can learn only from poems; to adopt talismanic models is to adopt postures, to import anxieties and other cultural curios.

In the 1960s cultural exchanges flourished. One can lament the passing of the great international festivals of poetry which brought onto one platform Giuseppe Ungaretti, John Ashbery, Pablo Neruda, Yves Bonnefoy, Peter Huchel, and Basil Bunting. Here were the big voices, some of them rusty and almost exhausted, speaking their own language; the relayed translation was an echo, it did not stand in for the thing itself. Yet the proliferation of published translations, most of them less than good, had its effect on poets. The piggy-back translation came of age: a poem could be translated from a crib. It was no longer necessary – it might not even be desirable – for the translator, so long as he was a poet, to know the language he was translating from. Translations which had in the past been acts of commitment by one individual writer to another became more casual, exercises to be conducted in workshops and a compulsory adjunct to literary festivals. The workshop poem, the workshop translation. . .

An international poetic language evolved, an eminently translatable esperanto of anecdote, image, gesture, poor in semantic resonance. Free verse – very free – became the norm. One began to feel, towards the end of those heady exchanges between European poets, that while Evgeny Evtushenko was performing his poems and exercising a tolerated dissidence in London, Manchester or Dublin, there were writers in the Soviet Union who were perhaps engaging their language, their tradition, and historical situation with greater precision and seriousness. The contemporary poetry that can be exported may not be the best but merely the most translatable in linguistic and political terms. Readers of modern poetry should discriminate between translated poets whose work exists in English – either because of the quality of the translations or despite it – and those who are ferried across the channel for other-than-poetic reasons.

As a publisher I was recently offered versions of a young German poet. Her translator outlined her career and her place within the German tradition, naming four German writers of the post-war years from whom she has taken direction. Only one of the four has been extensively translated in English. To publish this poet's work seemed to me a risk not worth taking – from her point of view as well as mine – since her poems (she is from East Germany) would inevitably be misread except by experts, who might as well read her in German. When English poetry readers have access to the larger figures from whom she has taken her bearings, it will be time to publish her.

If translation is to be of value to writers and readers, it must be possible for the *merely* subjective element in reading to be tempered not only by the provision of a 'critical context' for the translated writer, but by the wider availability of the informing texts. Anthologies are an important first step, but we are poorer in authoritative anthologies of non-English poetry now than we were a dozen years ago. The catholic European tradition still has a force for writers; but in the field of translated poetry a disoriented eclecticism reigns in publishers' lists and in bookshops, and critics find it difficult to place or advocate the work even of major figures because they suffer an inevitable ignorance which is more than merely philological. Sometimes it seems almost pathological, the Little Englandism for which Little England has become renowned since the Second World War. When Czeslaw Milosz and later Jaroslav Siefert were awarded the Nobel Prize for Literature, journalists and critics who had not heard of them and could not pronounce their names pronounced judgement, deriding the Sages of Stockholm for having celebrated 'unknown' foreigners.

10

They played the fool, not to appear as fools
In time's long glass. A deprecating air
Disarmed, they thought, the jeers of later schools;
Yet irony itself is doctrinaire,

And curiously, nothing now betrays
Their type to time's derision like this coy
Insistence on the quizzical, their craze
For showing Hector was a mother's boy.

A neutral tone is nowadays preferred.
And yet, it may be better, if we must,
To praise a stance impressive and absurd
Than not to see the hero for the dust.

Donald Davie, 'Remembering the 'Thirties'

Those of us engaged in the business of poetry publishing know
from the submissions we receive that many people read to get
a feel for the market and to imitate what they think will sell;
others read only what fuels their own Muse or consume only
the poetry that casts light upon the causes they support. Few
set out to find what Robert Frost in a corny and useful phrase
called 'the panhandle of poetry'. Few read without ulterior or
utilitarian motive. Self-enrichment, the unbankable enrichment
that follows from engagement and self-effacement, is the oldest
– and now among the rarest – of readerly motives. Derek
Walcott, in the poem which invokes 'the greatest reader in the
world', says of the art of reading:

> At least it requires awe,
> which has been lost to our time,
> so many people have seen everything,
> so many people can predict,
> so many refuse to enter the silence

of victory, the indolence
that burns at the core,
so many are no more than
erect ash, like the cigar,
so many take thunder for granted.
How common is the lightning,
how lost the leviathans
we no longer look for!

('Volcano')

Awe is what Milton felt for Spenser and Gunn felt for Keats. Our age, the age of 'imaginary museums' in which things are 'relative' and all literatures, past and present, are available to us, finds awe as difficult as belief. It has lost hunger for 'the silence', and with it the language with which to talk about the hunger. There is no time for the feverish indolence that makes the reader wise.

Critics with an axe to grind take poems as instances. They introduce them into debates about the Modern, and argue by fragmentation and by drawing sharp contrasts, as though opposed ideologies, life-styles, and formal choices made *types* of poetry different in kind. For us, the most humane and eloquent (though not the first) critic of this kind – himself the greatest poet of his period – is Matthew Arnold. Lesser critics follow. Poetry has been a *multum in parvo* of this conflict. Arguments about poetry can be extended from considerations of syntax, diction, metrical or free form, register and so on, into the wider battlegrounds of cultural (and political) ideology.

Contemporary critics have portrayed a 'two cultures' gulf between the popular poetry of public performance and what they take as more traditional modes; or between British and American; or Modernist and anti-Modernist; or male and female. This reductive technique is a clarifying, even a useful point of departure. The problem is the binary form, and the fact that major writers are often outside the categories proposed. In recent years the binary form has given way to more subtilized, if not more subtle, definitions in terms of region, nation, class, party, ethnic or sexual group. The approach depends upon establishing categories and then defining poems (or more usually poets) in terms of those categories, many of them remote from the actual words and processes of the poems.

It should be possible, I believe, to define a poetic tradition which includes the best poems of Philip Larkin and William Carlos Williams, of Roy Campbell and John Ashbery, of Elizabeth Bishop and W. S. Graham. I appreciate that the terms are already loaded: there is the vexatious word 'best' and the insistence on 'poems' rather than poetry: a value judgement allied to specific works which precedes generalizations. And there is the word 'tradition', which begs a thousand questions. How – after Modernism – can we speak of a continuous tradition? Tradition is surely unstable, too, given the ways in which our preferences change, so that we value Wyatt where Surrey was valued before, or now prefer Donne to Jonson. Is the Mexican poet Octavio Paz not right when he identifies a 'tradition of discontinuity' in our century, an 'alternating current'?

Paz is right in the European and Latin American contexts; and yet I believe his analysis is wrong for English-language poetry, where – for reasons I do not fully understand, though they have something to do with the bastard nature of our language – Modernism has gone shopping most fruitfully not in the markets of disruption or primitivism but in the rich markets of its own past, suddenly reviving Donne, Webster, Swift, Skelton, Doughty, Clough, or Smart. When English poetry has been energized by radicalism from abroad, it has applied it to its own roots and discovered precedents of its own.

In the poems of Tennyson's early maturity, written under the eye of Arthur Hallam, we have a great Symbolist poet before the event; passages in Shakespeare, Milton, Smart, and Beddoes (to name but a few) are consistently 'surreal' without an '–ism' being required. The '–ism' of Vorticism or Imagism and the rest have been added by assertive young writers in their apprenticeships, trying to draw attention to their work by inventing a movement and to signal radical departures. But they are departures from dominant conventions, not from the nurturing traditions – or so at least they prove as the writers move beyond the imitation of Continental strategies and mature

81

in different 'native' directions. Our '–isms' have, for the most part, been hybrid or imported: Modernism is Anglo-American or Anglo-Irish, never simply Anglo. Each movement, whatever the source, has been a phenomenon of re-appropriation and re-selection rather than rejection.

Tradition with its latent resources includes assumptions or values that diminish, by contrast as it were, the poems of Kingsley Amis and Robert Creeley, Earle Birney and Peter Redgrove, Sylvia Plath and Dylan Thomas. Reading is acquisitive; the good reader assimilates what is good; his memory is vulnerable to the best and stores it up; and as his reading improves so his sense of value and the keenness of his response are proven. Wide reading licenses us to select and to forget, to shed what becomes stale or small as we sharpen our art of reading.

I would not be so bold as to assert (though I confess I believe) that this tradition has an objective character. Because of the ways in which poets have used it, returning to the same fountainheads generation after generation, it seems to be much more stable than a consensus of subjectivities would be. It is expressed in unique works, but it remains Protean, like the *Geist* that German writers used to talk about, and to feel – as Gottfried Benn felt in an eloquent, elegiac passage – that once one starts trying to define it, it ceases to empower. It is not impossible that, in a world of commercial imperatives coupled with critical and cultural indirection, the tradition may be questioned or cajoled out of sight, though given the works that constitute it, it is likely to revive from time to time in further works, if only the forces of commercialism can be bribed to neglect it.

Since the 1930s, when political concerns grew so pressing as to make poets self-appointed spokesmen for causes and poetry 'occasional' in a very specific sense, the majority of poets have rejected certain kinds of writing and lines of approach. It is not uncommon, as we have seen, for writers (and readers) to reject the Anglo-American and Anglo-Irish Modernists on political grounds. Since the 1950s the purchase of Modernism has been weakened. Indeed, it had already appeared a little tenuous in the 1930s: dominant voices of the decade undertook formal experiments which, set beside the radical experimentation of early Eliot, of Pound, Joyce, Lewis, and Ford appear inessential. Eliot's own development as a writer may have helped to deflect the impact of his early work.

And since the 1970s pragmatism, literalism, a knowing dedication to the plausible, have come to dominate not only political but imaginative life as well. As I suggested at the outset, when one tries to identify 'religious poets', or poets for whom the various metaphysical concerns that shaped Housman, Hardy, and Hopkins are still real, it is hard to name more than a handful – R. S. Thomas, C. H. Sisson, Donald Davie, Elizabeth Jennings, Geoffrey Hill – for whom the presence or absence of Christian verities (which were a base-note of poetry through to the Second World War) retain imaginative reality.

Somehow, significant literary work continues, often beyond the market-place, the givens of journalism and personal anecdote, the poverty of formal resource and critical expectation. The least deliberately conspicuous poets can carry the tradition. If we want to find it, we must take account of poets generally considered 'difficult', and of poets who do not – and cannot – make themselves available to readers by methods which are increasingly those of efficient marketing.

There is nothing wrong with setting out to be the 'greatest reader in the world'. It is not a higher, though it can be a harder vocation than being a writer. It involves self-effacement, a craving for what extends understanding of the medium of language, and an aversion to usages, sentimentalities, and excesses which blur and impoverish expression. The task is difficult because no right or wrong is given outside the poem. What makes 'right' is the achieved poem, whatever it says, however sympathetic or repugnant the attitudes of the poet. In our tradition many elements are given, but not as dogma; and those elements justify themselves only in rare combination. Each combination is new or it is nothing. The demands a reader makes of a poem are passionate and severe. The demands a good poem makes on the reader are so various, so enriching, that the poem remains new on each reading.

83

11

'Established' is a good word, much used in garden books,
'The plant, when established' . . .
Oh, become established quickly, quickly, garden!
For I am fugitive, I am very fugitive –

Those that come after me will gather roses,
And watch, as I do now, the white wistaria
Burst, in its sunshine, from the pale green sheath.

Planned. Planted. Established. Then neglected,
Till at last the loiterer by the gate will wonder
At the old, old cottage, the old wooden cottage,
And say, 'One might build here, the view is glorious;
This must have been a pretty garden once.'

Mary Ursula Bethell, 'Time'

Coleridge contrasts the excesses of older poets with the very
different excesses of his contemporaries. What he says has a
curious appositeness for our time.

> Our faulty elder poets sacrificed the passion and passionate
> flow of poetry to the subtleties of intellect and to the starts of
> wit; the moderns to the glare and glitter of a perpetual yet
> broken and heterogeneous imagery, or rather to an
> amphibious something, made up half of image and half of
> abstract meaning. The one sacrificed the heart to the head,
> the other both heart and head to point and drapery.
>
> (*Biographia Literaria*: 117)

'Point and drapery' suggests not only decorative elements but
formal and tonal properties. Coleridge is issuing a still timely
warning against the plausible and facile, what the market may
want, what the age demands – a mould in plaster, as Pound
puts it,

. . . not, not assuredly alabaster,
Or the 'sculpture' of rhyme.
('Hugh Selwyn Mauberley')

There is a poetry that, like popular journalism, answers to the tastes of its day, and another kind which is unfamiliar (even when it is written in apparently conventional forms) and radicalizes taste and expectation. If the tastes of today are more and more determined by marketing and by journalistic criticism, in the past they were shaped by an insistence on applying conventions 'authorized' by a rather narrowly defined canon. The absurd Pindarics of the seventeenth and eighteenth centuries can be set against the miraculous emergence of Thomas Gray's great poems from an imagination which was more a collation of classical and approved English snippets than an independent integrative faculty. The same – to a lesser degree – might be said of A. E. Housman, and in different ways of David Jones and, in our own time, Geoffrey Hill.

Tradition can be tyrannical, but the poet who masters the tyrant brings away incomparable laurels. His struggle can be unavailing for years, and then suddenly he writes a poem for which it seems the tradition has been waiting. Or he writes agonizingly slowly, weighing every word with obsessive care until the balance is precise. Occasionally his resistances break down and there is a time of fluency, a miraculous (brief) freedom which allows him to write, for example, 'The Pentecost Castle'. But even here Geoffrey Hill might tell us that the sequence of three-quatrain lyrics took years to compose, the miraculous balladic lucidity being a triumph of labour and art as great as that expended upon his elaborate sonnet sequences.

In our time poetry has developed a closer relationship with polemical and prescriptive criticism than is healthy for it. When, for instance, the American critic M. L. Rosenthal described Robert Lowell's *Life Studies* (1956) as 'confessional poetry', the epithet was taken up as a licence by other poets. They felt liberated into 'confessing' in ways which had little to do with Lowell's process of mythologizing and delimiting his culture through select incidents from his and his family's history. When the 'deep image' was identified in the late 1960s, some poets in their forties who had been writing competent and sometimes eloquent formal verse departed with relief into what T. E. Hulme would surely have called the 'circumambient gas', plumbing their subconsciouses for imagery which might play upon our deepest common feelings. To the argument, 'This is incomprehensible!' they replied, 'precisely'. When in 1962 A. Alvarez suggested the 'gentility principle', which he quite plausibly saw as limiting the range of contemporary British poetry, he inadvertently gave rein to an anti-gentility movement that became commonplace in Britain during the 1960s and 1970s and is still with us today.

But it is not so much the old-fashioned critics, who seem to take their bearings from that most excellent of modern anthologists Michael Roberts, who do the damage. Their observations, categories, and epithets are the result of a close engagement with actual poems. They possess an historical sense and they have had the talent to identify some of the salient writers of their time before those writers were turned into Himalayas by later critics and publicists. It is the more deliberately theoretical critics who have effected lasting change – or done lasting damage – to reading and writing. Structuralists and post-structuralists and the critics who have grown out of them have various desiderata which they project and which some poets supply. The work of the American poet John Ashbery has been welcomed by a number of them, and its celebrity has spawned imitators who lack Ashbery's natural obliquity, his skill at orchestrating the elements in his memory into a texture of contrasting tones and voices which are sometimes heartbreaking and wry in one breath. His poetry does not lack content in the way that his celebrators suggest: it has a content that, like the poetry of Herrick, or of Keats, or of Wallace Stevens, is registered on the pulse. It is a poetry of tones, but those tones are specific and 'true'. Few of his contemporaries or his followers possess his tact, his aural memory and mimetic talent, or his skills at ventriloquism which make it possible for him to integrate disparate modes and styles in a single poem. His example is perilous because it has attracted the wrong sort of critical acclaim. He has been made a centrepiece at a post-modern feast when in fact he is a brilliant, iconoclastic Romantic for whom 'point and drapery' are a point of departure, not of arrival.

Ashbery's influence on American (and some British) poetry is comparable to the deleterious effect of Philip Larkin's presence in Britain. Larkin has been traduced into a kind of shaman for modern English poetry: a spell against Anglo-American Modernism, a validation of conventional forms and procedures. Yet his advocates can devalue his solitary individuality by portraying it as an irreducible 'modern condition'. Larkin is so distinctively Larkin that imitations of his work are immediately identifiable. He cannot be pillaged but stands as singly in the poetry of our time as Goldsmith does in the poetry of the eighteenth century. Like Goldsmith he has an immediately familiar aspect, disarming and approachable: he is an original miraculously delivered to us by a tradition which, for his emulators, is received as a series of mechanical conventions. They take point and drapery from him, without the firm thematic and formal engagement that characterizes his approach. The Mexican poet Octavio Paz lamented the insularity of Larkin, but then quoted two lines of his verse and forgave him everything.

One thing that makes Larkin's – like Ashbery's – work strangely impregnable is the way in which it parodies itself, its tones and attitudes. Larkin's irony is self-critical and self-adjusting, a function of his integrity. His imitators pick up the effects, the two-word paradoxes that undermine a flight of rhetoric, the irony of manner. But they cannot appropriate the tone, it is too distinctive, too slippery.

The laborious, deliberative approach of self-styled post-Modernist poets, who learn at a tangent from Pound or, more obliquely, from Barthes, can seem to justify those who value Larkin as antidote. So can the excesses of the English 'expressionists' of the 1960s and the experimentalists – Concrete and Sound poets – much of whose work is challenging to the critic and to fellow poets, but appears now to belong very much to its historical moment. Against these experiments and imitative excesses we can set the assimilative response of Davie and Gunn to the work of Pound, or of Hill to the work of Eliot, or of Heaney to the work of Joyce. Their distrust of critical prescription helps us appreciate the distinction between poets who find occasions rather than pretexts in earlier poetry, and poets who set out to manufacture a product for critical and eventual market consumption.

The American poet Hart Crane wrote to Harriet Monroe, the editor of *Poetry* (Chicago) in 1926, attempting to justify a poem he had submitted. He establishes the legitimacy of what he has written in relation to tradition in a way which casts light on the genuine integrative faculty:

> You ask me how a *portent* can possibly be wound in a *shell*. Without attempting to answer this for the moment, I ask you how Blake could possibly say that 'a *sigh* is a *sword* of an Angel King.' You ask me how *compass, quadrant and sextant 'contrive'* tides. I ask you how Eliot can possibly believe that 'Every street *lamp* that I pass *beats* like an a fatalistic *drum*!' Both of my metaphors may fall down completely. I'm not defending their actual value in themselves; but your criticism of them in each case was levelled at an illogicality of relationship between symbols, which similar fault you must have either overlooked in case you have ever admired the Blake and Eliot lines, or have there condoned them on account of some more ultimate convictions pressed on you by the impact of the poems in their entirety.
>
> It all comes to the recognition that emotional dynamics are not to be confused with any absolute order of rationalized definitions; ergo, in poetry the *rationale* of metaphor belongs to another order of experience than science, and is not to be limited by a scientific and arbitrary code of relationships either in verbal inflections or concepts.
>
> (*Complete Poems and Selected Letters*: 236–7)

The expression 'emotional dynamics' – rather like what Eliot meant when he described the German poet Hölderlin's poems as 'continuous metaphors for an emotion' – makes the distinction: it is something inherent in the poem, not something that can be contrived or, by the critic, extrapolated from it. It is inseparable from the process of writing (and of reading).

Donald Davie quotes a vulnerable note he wrote to himself in 1957:

> It is true that I am not a poet by nature, only by inclination; for my mind moves most easily and happily among abstractions, it relates ideas far more readily than it relates experiences. I have little appetite, only profound admiration, for sensuous fullness and immediacy; I have not the poet's need of concreteness. I have resisted this admission for so long, chiefly because a natural poet was above all what I wanted to be, but partly because I mistook my English empiricism for the poet's concreteness, and so thought my mind was unphilosophical whereas it is philosophical but in a peculiarly English way.
>
> (*Collected Poems 1950–1970*: 301–2)

Critics have used this hostage to fortune with a degree of malice, as Davie must have known they would. 'He stands condemned out of his own lips.' But Davie was too harsh with himself here: after all, he had written the astonishing early poems included in *A Winter Talent* (1957). Indeed, he sells short the excellences of his first collection, *Brides of Reason* (1955), with its eloquently tendentious title. Yet with the excessive harshness Davie always applies to his own work – the harshness of a man who feels he has not yet achieved the work that he was born to do – comes an insight into the effects of the English empiricism I tried to describe before, which closes out whole registers of feeling from modern English verse. It is a disability that most of Davie's contemporaries and successors suffer from, though they conceal it, either because they do not know they have it, or because they do not want us to know.

It is worth following Davie further in his confession because in describing what his poems are not, he finds and *wills* the direction he will take (and has taken in some of the best poems of our time) and that could be exemplary to other poets if they mustered the determination and mastered the skills that Davie has.

Most of the poems I have written are not natural poems, in one sense not truly poems, simply because the thought of them could have been expressed – at whatever cost in terseness and point – in a non-poetic way. This does not mean however that they are worthless, or that they are shams; for as much can be said of much of the poetry of the past that by common consent is worth reading and remembering. Nevertheless I have taken a decision to write no more poems of this kind, only poems which are, if not *naturally*, at all events *truly* poems throughout.

For a true poem can be written by a mind not naturally poetic – though by the inhuman labour of thwarting at every point the natural grain and bent. This working against the grain does not damage the mind, nor is it foolish; on the contrary, only by doing this does each true poem as it is written become an authentic widening of experience – a truth won from life against all odds, because a truth in and about a mode of experience to which the mind is normally closed.

(*Collected Poems 1950–1970*: 302)

Davie may be a little over-earnest in the passage. Once we have made allowance for his youth and for the fact that he was clarifying something for himself, and shared it with us only fifteen years later, we ought to apply what he says. This insight into his own work can be turned around: it is an astringent critical tool. Davie never quite kept to his resolve: he did write 'more poems of this kind' – his splendid *Six Epistles to Eva Hesse* for example. But he kept most of his promise and went on through the *Essex Poems* to his most 'natural' work in *In the Stopping Train* and (in another sense natural) *To Scorch or Freeze: Poems about the Sacred*. And there is the unique achievement of this 1957 resolution which was initially deliberate but became second nature to him: *Three for Watermusic*. What I admire particularly about Davie is his candour in admitting us to the process of his poetry and sharing with us the severest of his own self-censures. This is 'confessionalism' of the tallest order for a poet: it deserves attentive readers even though it inevitably attracts facile critical dismissals. It is confession within and about the *art* of his poetry, which is what matters.

Hart Crane is like Davie in his resolution and openness, if in little else. In the letter to Harriet Monroe which I quoted before, he writes: 'as long as poetry is written, an audience, however small, is implied, and there remains the question of an active or an inactive imagination as its characteristic'. It is with the active imagination that he sought to engage, the imagination familiar with Eliot, Blake and their wider context. It is by active imagination that poems are produced and poems are read in something more than a subjective fashion, if they are read at all.

When his poem is finished – or abandoned – a poet believes he has made a statement, enacted a process or completed an experience which, properly and sensitively approached, will inform, affect, or act upon a reader in a specific way. A teacher, by contrast, may claim that there are as many readings of a poem as there are readers. Obviously the teacher is right: each reader 'is read' differently by a poem, is touched or troubled by different nuances, has a deeper or less assured semantic sense, hears rhythmic echoes or because of accent or some other accident is deaf to the sound of the poem. But the teacher is right only to a degree. If the effect of the poem is *finally* subjective, if the reader cannot get beyond the private *frisson* of, say, applauding the poet's meaning, or hearing some string of his own memory plucked by an image or cadence, then the poem has failed, or the reader has failed the poem. Poetry is not – as the refrain of my essay insists – preaching to the converted; it aims to give pleasure, but the pleasure it gives is radical, not conventional, and should take the reader beyond that subjectivity of response at which teachers may feel inclined to stop.

There is in any reader who loves poetry, and not just the clutch of poems that he loves, a discrimination (whether he articulates it as such or not) between what he genuinely likes and what he recognizes to be good even though he does not like it. It is a distinction between taste and judgement, the latter a kind of sherpa to the former, guiding it up the mountain. For my part, I have disliked Blake and, earlier, Hopkins as poets. My dislike did not affect the value of their work. I was able to teach it with conviction because I sensed its qualities. I learned rather more from it than I did from, say, the poems of George Herbert or of Edward Thomas which I loved excessively. Judgement gradually opened out taste and overcame a subjective lack of appreciation. Had I followed first instincts 'The Book of Thel' would have remained closed to me, and with it the ability to read Blake's more eloquent heirs with any degree of understanding. 'Good taste must be acquired,' says my favourite teacher Coleridge, 'and like all other good things, is the result of thought and the submissive study of the best models.' The kind of 'thought' and 'submissive study' that Coleridge speaks of has little to do with classrooms and much to do with the self-creative reading which takes place in privacy and tends not towards acquisition and utility but towards understanding. Coleridge's language often has a fervent, almost religious tenor.

Another tentative distinction is useful in an age when the majority of poets make their livings within the academic world: the distinction between *learned* and *cultured* poets. For many, learning is a matter of acquisition, collation, and arrangement, and they are concerned to place themselves within a tradition. But there are those poets for whom their culture is second nature, who give the impression of having been born to it and have little time for prescriptive criticism. Impassioned readers, they are reluctant to establish the 'objective' or the 'judicial' approach of the academic teacher and critic, preferring to write a criticism which refuses to attenuate its healthy prejudices and which – to the annoyance of the *learned* – tolerates a degree of misquotation (quotation from memory). They will not play at a 'fair-mindedness' which can lead to bland tolerance. They make good teachers, but not in the classroom. Burns Singer went to Madron in Cornwall to sit at the feet of W. S. Graham, who must have been the most cantankerous and illuminating of teachers. Singer camped in a tent in the garden.

Perhaps this is again Davie's distinction between writers who are *naturally* poets and writers who, after considerable struggle against the grain, overcome their native empiricism and become *truly* poets. Charles Tomlinson in one poem has 'Chopin shaking music from the fingers' – a paradigm for the first kind of poet; while Tomlinson himself – even in that brief quote, with the deliberation of the definite article – is one of the finest examples we have of the second kind.

12

Unwisely I have read
Sartre on Imagination – very dry, very French,

An old hound with noises in his head
Who dreams the hunt is on, yet fears the stench

Of action – he teaches us that human choice
Is rarely true or kind. My children are asleep.

James K. Baxter, 'The Buried Stream'

The poet, not the publisher, teacher or reader, makes the poem. The poem may be a window on the age, it may illuminate or satirize some aspect of its time or its occasion, but such effects are, *sub specie aeternitatis*, incidental to its enduring, intransitive presence. If it surprises us with rhythm or with wisdom, this is evidence that the poet has learned something of his art in creating it.

Yet authentic poems find their place in tradition and are not entirely comprehensible outside it. Each poet is to some degree *doctus*. Each poem is unique in itself and in its complex relationship with its antecedents and the world. We learn most not from the relevance of a poem – what it says to us about contemporary issues – but from its irrelevance, the extension of understanding it offers. And while a poem may increase our understanding of science, politics, or the human heart, it will in the first place extend our understanding of the potentialities of our language in its most specialized and expressive usage.

The sense of a poem is the product of the poet's experience of language (itself inseparable from the poet's experience of life, but also from his experience of other poetry). It is a play of energies, and a poet whose approach to language remains imitative of other writers' usage will be unable to release those energies. Alice Meynell made a distinction between vivacity and genuine vitality in prose fiction, between a language of social energy and a language of imaginative energy. It is the distinction we can apply to poetry, discriminating between the work of Kingsley Amis and that of Philip Larkin, between metaphors of Craig Raine and those of Norman MacCaig.

The poem has form, and form is not synonymous with the anecdotal structure called 'narrative' which is now popular, or stanza shape or rhyme-scheme. It has to do with semantics, with the relations between words, with dynamics of rhythm, metre and rhyme and the syntheses that the poet achieves, in which many meanings choose one word-complex and are harmonized, even in contrast and contradiction, within one imaginative structure. In an achieved poem, form is never merely mechanical, even if the formal choice is something as apparently schematic as a sonnet. If the poem works, it is hard to discuss (though one can describe) form separately from the energies it integrates. Seamus Heaney in a recent discussion insisted:

> a sonnet, for example, isn't fourteen lines that rhyme; a sonnet is a system of muscles and enjambements and age and sex, and it's got a waist and a middle – it is a form . . . there are indeed fourteen lines and there are indeed rhyme words at the end, but the actual movement of the stanza, the movement of the sonnet isn't there. I would like a distinction between form which is an act of living principle and shape which is discernible on the page, but inaudible, and kinetically, muscularly unavailable. Poetry is a muscular response also, I feel. If you read a Shakespeare sonnet, a beloved Shakespeare sonnet, it's a dance within yourself.
>
> (BBC Radio 4, 'Kaleidoscope',
> printed in *PN Reviews* 66 (1989))

Heaney's lively and fanciful description is a timely corrective to the increasingly masonic 'new formalists' both in Britain and abroad who welcome a rhyme or a metrical stanza as a coded handshake and talk of *craft* as though the art of poetry were a kind of carpentry. It isn't. Skills are required, but skills, materials, tools, and a good work-bench do not ensure that the end product will be a poem.

Poems change and increase on each reading, and a real poem cannot be exhausted by study or analysis. It is not that it withholds something from us; it has no 'hidden meaning' but a wealth of implicit meaning: it continues giving. Dante celebrates Love as the only commodity that increases the more it is given; a good poem is similarly a language of accrual, an inexhaustible resource.

Yet this quality is the last to be highlighted by those who set out to 'raise the profile of poetry' in advertising promotions, who treat poetry as a product and speak of markets. Indeed the inexhaustible resource, like the indestructible washing machine, is bad for business. Readers must be hurried along to the next sensation. The market must be kept agitated – not hungry, exactly, but curious. Curious about the *news* of poetry, the exotic poet, the event. Poetry – as I have suggested – is sold short as soon as talk of readers is supplanted by talk of markets. 'Product' becomes homogenized, and the originality is in the packaging.

There is a huge market for poetry today – the academic market at all levels. The very institutions which provide so many writers with employment consume the product of their vocation: a splendid ecological model. If one identifies, for example, Vernon Scannell as a useful classroom text in primary schools, it is because some of his poems – not necessarily the best ones – can be taken apart and put together again. They respond to basic critical approaches and concentrate on subjects which are, or are thought to be, appropriate for young readers. The poet and anthologist David Wright, a fine editor who despises the fashions and fashion-makers and distrusts the ways in which poetry has become an academic subject, has written of the 'identikit poem' that teachers rejoice to have in the classroom – not 'Imagine a Forest' by W. S. Graham but 'Digging' by Seamus Heaney. Patrick Kavanagh, whose central place in modern Irish poetry is at last justly acknowledged, largely thanks to Wright and latterly to Heaney, said: 'The aim of a good deal of literary and academic criticism is to raise up the mediocre, to get people to believe that the tenth-rate is somehow respectable.' Criticism of this kind is the handmaiden of marketing.

In the newspapers the most influential critics of poetry nowadays are – many of them – distinguished Professors of English with, to say the least, specialized tastes. There was a time when poets such as Edwin Muir, Donald Davie, John Heath-Stubbs, and (in another country) Randall Jarrell wrote as though the art mattered, and with a severe generosity which knew how to welcome the new.

Critics, especially of the academic kind with a taste for wit and banter, for the brave low talk of the high table, have certain habits: they see literature as a battle-ground rather than a *bourse*. They like categories, the shorthand which blurs distinctions between works. If they cannot take sides, they prefer to side-step a poem. This is not a new phenomenon. Coleridge commented upon 'the contempt with which the best-grounded complaints of injured genius are rejected as frivolous or entertained as matter for merriment' by those who make taste. They become so attuned to selected products of their age that the work of the past and the radical work of the present come to bore – or merely amuse – them. The brutal, unserious treatment of so seminal a poet as Laura Riding is evidence of this. Biographical curiosity runs far deeper than an interest in the poems. It is doubtful whether Robert Lowell ever earned as much from a book of his poems as his biographer earned from telling the colourful, sad story of his life. As reading becomes more subjective, interest in the poet's subjectivity grows. Literature is gossip. Some poets realize this and build their poems out of the kinds of trivia that fill a day. It is – or has been, for there are signs of impatience with the genre – the age of anecdote poems.

Readers who cannot get a perspective on the poems of our own time – and given the variety of work available, it can be difficult – may find their way by following certain thematic preferences, or a political line, or a formal predilection. Few can have the awe and tact of Edward Thomas who, when he first reviewed the work of a curious American *parvenu*, Ezra Pound, conceded that he had no language in which to address such work and apologized to Pound 'for our own shortcomings and to any other readers for that insecurity of modern criticism of which we feel ourselves at once a victim and a humble cause'. He was perplexed by a poetry written as though Shakespeare had not been, with a semantic and rhythmic freshness he could not assess.

The language of criticism can become autocthonous not only in the work of theorists but also in the writing of regular poetry reviewers. Publisher, poet and critic are a curious triangle. The publisher may edit a book, but his visible function is to establish the design, promotion and release, and to present the poet to the critical and promotional media. But the text is there, in black and white. And the critic fulfils – or not – his obligations. The reader has several hurdles to get over before the poems can get to work.

Coleridge quotes Sir Joshua Reynolds as saying: 'next to the man who formed and elevated the taste of the public, he that corrupted it is commonly the greatest genius.' The corrupting is more common than the elevating genius, especially in criticism where editors and reviewers can have vested interests. In their own age the two forms of genius are often confused with one another. Occasionally they combine in the same person. It is a matter of comfort to meet writers with 'the power of reconciling the two contrary yet co-existing propensities of all human nature, namely indulgence of sloth and hatred of vacancy'. Comfort, but not clarification. Books have declined, Coleridge suggests, from oracles to venerable preceptors to instructive friends to entertaining companions to (finally) 'culprits to hold up their hands at the bar of every self-elected yet not the less peremptory judge who chooses to write from humour or interest, from enmity or arrogance'. The critic rises as the author sinks, and the franchise of the critic, as any committed teacher knows, extends to the student who stands on the dignity of ignorance and regards 'I don't like it' as a satisfactory response to a poem, whether it is by Milton or Wendy Cope.

Most readers start from ignorance, but those who aspire to become *great readers* do not suffer from arrogance. Literary critics are no different. Critics should give an account of their growth, the personal tradition that they embody. Coleridge is again a paradigm. In *Biographia Literaria* he is at pains to remember when he first came across Wordsworth's work, for example; he traces the progress of his understanding, of their collaboration and eventual estrangement. It is the story of a relationship between two men, but more compellingly a debate between two imaginations at one time closely attuned in apprenticeship, yet radically dissimilar in direction and temperament.

Sometimes in reading Dr Johnson's *Lives of the Poets*, or Arnold's essays, or the writings of Sainte-Beuve, or Randall Jarrell's classic reviews, an important element is missing: a sentence or two of autobiography, a succinct confession that places the critic in relation to the subject. How familiar is the critic with the subject? If critics write of a contemporary, are they acquainted? Do they belong to the same college, the same club? Do they endorse similar causes? Dr Johnson's comment on King Lear's 'Undo this button' is so helpful because it defines Johnson's attitude (and that of his age) to decorum, and it helps the reader to qualify Johnson's arguments with a *specific* understanding of the critic.

When Eliot embarks on an essay on Dante (as the Italian poet Eugenio Montale declares), he ought to say how much Italian he knows, whether it is merely a text-book facility, whether he knows the context of Dante's work and the writing of his contemporaries, how familiar he is with the 'patristics' of criticism and interpretation that have assimilated the work to different ages. In short, especially with critics whose style is magisterial and discriminating, it is important to know how much of our trust they merit. True: when we read Eliot on Dante we are learning about Eliot, and if he makes mistakes because of a faulty grasp of Italian or of Dante's context, he still illuminates his subject. But there are not many Eliots.

How can we be sure of a critic? If the criticism is invigorating? Yet some dazzling criticism today is an exercise in style at something of a tangent to the texts it pretends to interpret. Harold Bloom's fanciful eloquence – when it is comprehensible – can be illuminating, yet time after time, at the expense of the text, it calls on us to admire the critic's subtlety. His writing longs to become a text in its own right. Even as we are startled by what Sartre tells us when his subject is Genet or what Barthes tells us when his occasion is Racine, we may feel uneasy at the distance between the critic and the works as we apprehend them, and feel the critic has had other fish to fry, that Genet and Racine have been pretexts. Genet certainly felt this way when he read Sartre's essay. He had become a clause in one of Sartre's bigger arguments.

My distrust of criticism as of publishing has much to do with its sins of omission. Those sins have the effect of impoverishing the reader. In an age in which there is no literary consensus and no critical *lingua franca*, the young reader hungry for new work takes direction from critic and bookseller. In the interests of trade there must be 'market leaders'. An impression of coherence is created. Critics establish categories, groupings, and 'schools', publishers generate the product, and booksellers oblige the reading public. The tyranny of the anthology has never, since the heyday of Palgrave, been so great as it is now, even as the exploitation by publishers and agents of copyright fees diminishes the range and quality of introductory volumes.

It is only during the last three decades that the market for modern poetry has become significant and targetable, as a result of developments in curricula. Whatever the poet's aspirations may be, the publisher aspires to have books on the syllabus. I speak as a publisher. Yet as writer and editor I'm not content with the way the reader is served – or with the way the reader is trained and directed. Inherent in the publishing industry and in the current educational system is a loss of historical perspective. In one A Level syllabus students are given a choice between reading Chaucer, Milton, Wordsworth, or Elizabeth Jennings. Such a list is meaningless: it takes poetry as a sufficient category in itself. One might as well set a Prose Syllabus in which students can choose between Sir Thomas Browne, Sterne, Gibbon, D. H. Lawrence, or Angela Carter.

My ideal reader prefers poetry to criticism. What arrests him is the poem, and in valuing it he will follow Coleridge's suggestion, assessing what the poet has set out to do, how well it is done, and finally whether it was worth doing. The quality of

101

expression, its consistency and authority as witness in language, detain him. This reader can be identified and encouraged in a classroom, but only the best teacher can create him.

Reading Modern Poetry seems to have become less a work of description than a confession. The saddest part of the confession is this: I begin to feel that Eliot was not wrong when he said that the editor finds it difficult to acknowledge new talent as he grows older; at 40 his creative discrimination – the ability to judge the work of his juniors – becomes impaired. While I still warm to the work of some writers in their twenties, I find my enthusiasm uncertain. Yvor Winters counselled against enthusiasm as a critical attitude. It involves a squandering of emotion and leads to misvaluation, distortion of the truth, self-deception. Winters, of course, was not a publisher. But he was an acute reader, and I doubt that he would have approved of the work of his British publisher. Certainly he would not have tolerated the attempt of a publisher to steal time from making and selling books in order to set out in general terms how he approaches modern poetry, and to suggest how others might find a way in a neon-lit republic of letters. I do have vested interests, like any businessman; yet the enthusiasms I act on are not commercial but editorial, and those enthusiasms have much to do with my sense that readers have lacked certain crucial resources.

Poets need a context, and that context is provided by criticism (which clears a space for them) and by readers (who engage their work at the most basic levels) and by the availability of texts drawn from the wider tradition which inform and relate to their work. If criticism lets them down, if readers are shy, if the wider tradition is available only in libraries and second-hand bookshops, poets find the way more stony than necessary.

13

Irony does not save:
The knowledge that you repeat
The infantile indiscreet
Reactions of the dead

Does not save. Irony
Says nothing when her hand
Gestures the promised land.
Irony is the dead

Who are not saved but see
Magnificent bold Orpheus
Claim the incredulous
Soon-to-return Eurydice.

Dick Davis, 'Irony and Love'

The major New Zealand poet James K. Baxter was driven to spiritual and social excesses by the unresponsiveness of the literary culture that surrounded him. He had no peers, whether friends or foes, in his imaginative neighbourhood. That is one explanation of what went wrong for him, more plausible than blaming the 1960s, that scapegoat decade. In his last years it would seem that he had disciples and acolytes rather than readers. I know too little of his social world, and I do not wish to question the sincerity of his lonely late faith in the *Jerusalem Sonnets*; I do wonder, though, whether the world he was born into was not unequal to the originality of his work and unresponsive to his needs. Did he waste his best talents in attempting to find in metaphysics, among the Maoris, in the miasma of his last decade, a validation that his own cultural environment had denied him? Readers failed him at home and abroad – failed in the reciprocity that some poets require to give them balance and context. Emily Dickinson needed Higginson, however limited his response to her work may seem to us today; and Hopkins needed Robert Bridges. Baxter seems to have lacked even a Higginson, a Bridges. He deserved better than he got.

The same question can be asked about poets whose cases were not so extreme as his: about Basil Bunting, John Berryman, and Philip Larkin, for example. Robert Lowell once spoke of the terrible moment when a poet becomes too large for critics to challenge and criticize. At that point his poet friends have embarked upon their different journeys, too, and are either jealous and competitive, or have no time to take him to task for his mistakes, excesses, aberrations. He is met with adulation or hostility: 'The odds is gone.' For Lowell, that was the point at which the poet becomes most vulnerable. He must fall back entirely upon himself, and he is even more alone and exposed than he was when he set out. He must weigh his own work, and nothing is more difficult than that.

Perhaps writers are luckier today than Baxter was. If the Australian poet Les A. Murray found his native audience unresponsive, he would have readers in a wider English-speaking world in a way that Baxter, dying when the Provinces were written off as unimportant, did not do. And even when he found himself stolidly established in New South Wales, he would still be regarded cautiously, as a poet to be proven, in Britain, Canada, and the United States. The possibility of an international English-speaking audience prolongs the youth of some poets simply by giving them a variety of readerships, each with different cultures and interests. Charles Tomlinson when he found few readers in England developed an American following. Thom Gunn took the opportunity to emigrate to a community in California more congenial and supportive than the one he left behind. Some freedoms are more readily available – and not only to writers on private incomes – than they were.

For rare poets such as Robert Lowell, however, whose international reputations are established very early, there is not the same sense of new audiences to address when, around the age of 45, their careers enter their most vulnerable phase. It is at that stage that they most acutely need committed readers willing to call them to account. Readers are not only the consumers of literature: they are part of the context of living writers, and the reciprocity between writer and reader should transcend the purchase of books.

Ezra Pound was a poet whose cultural environments were not rigorous and responsive enough for him. Or rather, in his early years, when he was valuable to specific groups of young poets and to Yeats, Joyce, Ford, and others, he shaped a context, he orchestrated a series of dialogues, in which he taught and learned in equal degrees. But after *Mauberley*, when he 'abandoned the English' as Donald Davie puts it, moving to France and later to Italy, and as the writers he had worked with went their different ways, he became isolated. Like Ford Madox Ford, his generosity was ill-repaid. He remained a serious reader, critic, and friend of those he had helped, and he found new writers to encourage. But he was left on his own. In my view his politics (like those of Wyndham Lewis) are less culpable than his severest critics make them largely because of the irresponsibility of those who watched them develop and did not argue with him in a sustained and cogent way at the time. Perhaps his politics simply bored the writers who most liked his work, or they didn't have time to respond to his increasingly intemperate letters and articles. If this was the case, then they bear some of the responsibility for what 'went wrong' with his economic and political theories.

Criticism of Pound's poetry and prose has become a major industry. Biographies and biographical essays proliferate. Increasingly this literature is a monument of misunderstanding. The poems as living and informing texts are almost erased by it. A palisade of recondite exegesis and, latterly, of psychological and structuralist studies, blocks access. To some readers Pound is simply a pariah. The introductory work of Hugh Kenner and Donald Davie, from very different perspectives, still leads directly to the poet if the reader needs – as most modern readers believe they do – critics to ease the approach.

Many of the older British poets writing today – those born between 1914 and 1935 – have taken important bearings from Pound. Many of them have been marginalized in recent years by the forces which marginalized Pound and make him anathema to some of my generation. Many readers under the age of 45 feel justified in ignoring him altogether. They may be revolted by his political stance in the 1930s and 1940s. When this is the case, they are generally too hostile to take into account the earlier and later stances, the appalling testimony of the *Pisan Cantos*, or the space which his translations and criticism occupy. Rejection of Pound wholesale can be seen as one cause of the technical impoverishment of some recent poetry. A poet who takes Pound on board is unlikely to let himself off lightly. Some of the critical severity (and generosity) of writers as different as Bunting, Sisson, Gunn, Tomlinson, Davie, and Hill owes something to Pound.

Disproportionate critical attention is lavished on poetry which deliberately rejects the resources which Pound and the other Modernists made available in their poetry and criticism. There is a logic of consecutive argument which distrusts the associative, allusive logic of the imagination. There is a nationalist bias which sees Pound and the Modernists as alien to the English tradition; an ideological anxiety which sees Pound and his contemporaries only in the half-light of their political opinions; a very common commonsense which rejects the claims they made for the integrative imagination. There is also a populism which asserts that what is obscure – cultural references, the assumption that readers might have read, or might wish to read, Flaubert or Cavalcanti or Jefferson, the belief that readers have ears that can be attuned to something more expressive than the metronome – is elitist and that any allusion beyond the grasp of the man in the street is presumptuous. There is something treacherously democratic about all this: merit is established by a show of hands: the poet has a duty to address us in familiar terms. He is not allowed to explore or to hold obnoxious ideas.

Philip Larkin gave new currency, in a reductive spirit, to the pleasure principle in literature. We can subscribe to it if we insist that the greatest pleasures poetry gives are not those of first reading, and that sometimes the most rebarbative initiation results in the most vivid illuminations. Some readers find that

Larkin's work itself exemplifies this. There are other poets whose difficulties open the ear. In penetrable difficulty there is a value, an authority in irrelevance.

The English poet Christopher Middleton – long an exile in Texas, France, Germany, Anatolia, anywhere but Britain – addressed an open letter to the framers of an American educational training scheme. He describes the common prejudice in favour of 'relevance' in educational policy.

> There is much to be said for the efforts of Humanities teachers who try to make apparently remote matters 'relevant'. But here there is a serious problem. By reducing the otherness of other things, and those things may be texts, pictures, ideas, moral systems, for the sake of relevance, the teacher merely indulges existing egomorphic 'behavioral patterns'. The object of study, once its otherness is denied or ignored, is merely cut to fit the student's condition of mind, his existing frame of reference. No real intellectual transformation, no real structuring refinement of sensibility, no cultivation of instinct, can occur without exertion toward the other, which is the living nerve of both educational and spiritual disciplines. That is, at least, the story from Plato to Wittgenstein. If objects of study are no longer tended for what they are, as intrinsically interesting structures of meaning that can be shared, then they cease to radiate their interior life. The norms of teacher and student remain untransformed and eclipse all features other than those which suit the criteria offered by those norms. If those criteria are such as fail to identify what they cannot measure, and so fail to achieve intelligent contact with the *other reality*, then those criteria are wrong for the educational process.   (*Bolshevism in Art*: 145–6)

This passage speaks not only to the framers of curricula but to teachers, and to critics. 'If those criteria are such as fail to identify what they cannot measure. . .' We end up applying familiar templates to anything that is strange. We scale things down to fit them into our classrooms, our libraries, our critical essays. The process of education becomes a process of contraction, colonization, control.

The rule of 'I know what I like' results indulging 'existing egomorphic "behavioral patterns"'. It is inevitably a rule of cultural impoverishment and of arrogance. No reader is competent who cannot surrender to a poem. It may be that the surrender is not accepted, that the poem is too frail to command. But it must be given the chance on its own terms, the way that Edward Thomas gave Pound the chance and was extended by what he read.

It is worth remembering that Ezra Pound, in translating Anglo-Saxon, Chinese, Latin, Italian and other poetries into English, created in tone, diction, and cadence a sense of the otherness of the poetry translated, its rhetorical, linguistic and historical distance from his contemporary usage. And Christopher Middleton in his translations of Goethe insists on elements of syntax in his original, believing (correctly, it seems to me) that Goethe's exploitation of the potentialities of German word order was essential not only to his formal choices but to the meanings he intended to convey. Michael Hamburger's translations of Paul Celan, too, refuse to mask or to explicate the impacted complexities of the late poems.

Translations which read 'as if the poem was originally written in English' ought to give us pause. Romance languages are especially treacherous here. From the Spanish, for instance, versions of Pablo Neruda which deploy a strong monosyllabic vocabulary and fall back on the iambic foot are remote from their originals. The translator may believe he has found a cultural equivalence within the English tradition, and yet no such equivalence can exist for a poetry as remote from ours as that of Neruda, or Federico García Lorca or Octavio Paz, even when – as in the case of Paz – the poet has learned lessons from Pope and Wordsworth, Frost and Williams. The act of domestication is an act of forgery. The best translations do not assimilate originals to a present norm. Pound reacted strongly against the Victorianizing of Dante, Homer, and others. Robert Lowell had the candour to call his assimilative translations 'imitations'.

This insistence on *irrelevance*, on the illuminating distance between the familiar and the remote, relates back to the distinction I tried to draw between taste and judgement. It is a challenge to encompass a new language, a challenge to apprehend the literature of the eighteenth century, to engage Goldsmith, for example, in terms which restore his full expressiveness. Reading is an act of restoration as well as an act of construction: reading puts inflection, voice, and rhythm back into the printed text. If we dislike – because we find difficult – the conventions of the eighteenth century and reject them, we reject the poetry whose context they are. If we are disinclined to take on board the poets who drew their sustenance from Milton then we turn a deaf ear to a major harmony in our tradition. Reading is a form of cultivation which can start with study and deliberate application. It will become a deeper mastery, an instinct, as it is pursued.

Ted Hughes is, like every distinctive poet, free-standing. Yet between appreciation of his work (taste) and understanding (judgement) there remains a distance. It is possible to respond strongly to the work of a defined imagination like his or Larkin's; but without a sense of the elements which have gone into that definition, response may not involve understanding.

For years I have read the work of Wallace Stevens – especially the poems in *Harmonium* – with pleasure, taking his *Selected* with me on every vacation. I have tried to understand his work there only at a technical level, and my enthusiasm for Stevens is no more than that. My reticence before his 'meanings' has been defensive. Instinct warns me that the poems – so suggestive in tone and so rich in metaphor – conceal a vacancy, as though the work was a product of play, of temporizing over a void, and his inexaustible regularity fluttered an empty sleeve. Perhaps my instinct tells me that 'meanings' would diminish the poems.

As an undergraduate, I devoted months of study to *Four Quartets*. Eventually it struck me that the 'intolerable wrestle with words and meanings' had occurred in Eliot's early work. The *Quartets* were the product of a dramatist and an architect – not argument but argufying, subtilized and tenuous, a poetry reluctant to declare that it was made of prose meanings, another wonderfully embroidered empty sleeve. But what authority in the rhetoric, what subtlety in the extension of the ideas! Perhaps the language exceeds its occasion, as Eliot says that Kipling's does in some of his poems. In such cases, to understand the occasion may be to diminish the pleasure. And yet it may be that modern poets working on any scale at all must 'construct something upon which to rejoice', when nothing can be taken as given in theme, form, or readership.

14

The English that I feel in
Fears the inauthentic
Which invades it on all sides
Mortally. The style may die of it,
Die of the fear of it,
Confounding authenticity with essence.

Donald Davie, 'Epistle. To Enrique Caracciolo Trejo'

Reading contemporary poetry: but as we have seen, there are as many forms of reading as there are forms of poetry! The teacher reads in order to prepare a lesson; the student to pass an exam; the lecturer to ease overworked undergraduates around a text; the critic to write a review; the theorist to find tenants for his procrustean bed; the publisher to make decisions about investment; the editor to fill a poetry space in a journal; the politicized reader to confirm or extend ideological preferences; the journalist to determine the poet's personality; the adjudicator to award a prize; the aspiring writer to compete with the acceptable product of the day. For most readers of contemporary poetry the act of reading is transitive, not sacramental. Every reader performs an act of discrimination, but not necessarily an act of aesthetic discrimination.

Instrumental reading has always been with us, though in earlier ages to a lesser degree than now. The reader of contemporary poetry who comes to the text out of passionate curiosity and without ulterior motive is a rare bird. Most of us at least begin our reading life as rare birds; some manage to retain hunger and independence of judgement even within their vocations. But the deliberate uses to which poetry is put in education, social debate, and the market-place, make it difficult to read in the traditional sense, and this difficulty if it is not overcome is an impoverishment.

Yes: poets have politics, are endowed with gender, and

sometimes are self-serving. Readers are no different. Yet ours is an age of critical and readerly metonymy: the part stands for the whole. Poets with certain extra-poetic characteristics or concerns are celebrated or reviled. This is not an age of disinterested readers because it is not an age of free poets, despite the statistics and the generous provision of funding for writers, magazines and presses, despite public performances, secondments, conferences and fellowships. Despite – or because? Reading poetry, especially contemporary poetry, has become institutionalized, a communal activity. There is a syllabus, not a canon; a fashion, not a tradition. Judging from the number of 'writers' workshops' active around the country, writing poetry, too, can be a group activity. Peter Sansom evokes a 'session' in 'The Fox in the Writing Class':

> Now we are silent except for our pens
> and the teacher's intense questions. Above us
> the air-conditioning whirrs like fine drizzle on
> slumbering fern in a falling-dark pine-forest.
> My girlfriend enters in one of the lines
> but I know – sorry darling! – she will be
> erased in a later draft. . .

The act of reading for pleasure is different from the act of reading in order to teach. Reading submissions to a magazine is different from reading manuscripts for book publication. The disparity between these distinct kinds of reading leads me back to the conviction that the engaged reader of poetry must develop the double faculty of taste and judgement. I have remarked how as a teacher I taught Blake's poems with convic-tion even though I disliked them and what underlies them intensely. My dislike did not affect the quality of the work. With the poems of Wilfred Owen the balance is different. I know much of Owen's poetry by heart and love it, but when it comes to the function of judgement I have no choice but to judge it as faulted in its rhetoric and even dishonest in the terms it proposes, and inferior to work of Edward Thomas, Isaac Rosenberg and even, in some respects, of Siegfried Sassoon. Though I would sooner take Owen to a desert island,

I would argue that Rosenberg is the truer, and in some respects the nobler, poet.

If students of mine read the poems of Larkin and report that they dislike them, I'm not interested. They must come to terms with Larkin whether they like him or not. Judgement of a work cannot stop at self-judgement. 'I don't like it' is a way of shutting the eyes. There may be good reasons for disliking the poetry of Larkin. It is those reasons that the student must formulate and that the teacher waits to hear. Larkin cannot be 'written off' by a serious reader any more than Pound can. My dislike for Blake tells me something about my aesthetic and political preferences. It tells me very little about Blake. When I understand the complex perspectives of the 'Book of Thel', the conflict between Innocence and Experience which is as subtle and suggestive as the difference in similarity between Milton's 'L'Allegro' and 'Il Penseroso', I 'transcend myself'. What is required of the engaged reader is not a suspension of disbelief in the text but a suspension of belief in oneself. A breach, if you like, in our ingrained individualism, the 'I know what I like' which prevails among consumers of art. Engaged readers are not consumers only; and students, if they are consumers, are something less than the educational strategists have envisaged, and something less than those who go professionally into the teaching of literature bargained for.

Students who limit their choice from the smörgåsbord of ill-structured contemporary education only to what they like, what they find relevant, begin to indulge in a solipsism which circumscribes growth and development, self-limitation which the very concept of the Humanities set out to vanquish. Teachers and lecturers are partly responsible for encouraging these impoverishments, by tolerance of choice among the least experienced students, those not yet sufficiently trained, informed, educated, to choose.

If this period, rich in choices for poets and readers and yet poor in purpose and seriousness, is spoilt by tolerant indifference, earlier periods have had impoverishments too. With the Restoration and the intellectual and social revolutions that accompanied it, poetry became a language answering three primary demands: to instruct, celebrate or entertain. Whole registers of language and feeling came to seem inappropriate – among them the very registers which had sufficed the poets of the century before the Commonwealth, the 'noblest' period in our tradition, poets who matured before Hobbes saw the great darkness and Rochester felt it palpably smother him when he was not laughing for breath.

Poets began to become public figures, no longer sitting at the king's table but competing for a living among secular patrons, in the ale house or, worse, in the academy or, worse still, in the market-place. Poets were held – or held themselves – to account. Their utterances were restricted to areas in which it was deemed proper for them to work, and they produced what the age demanded unless, by very force of character and skill, they created a demand for what they wished to write. A decorous language evolved which was held appropriate – strictly so – for the different kinds of poetic statement. The poetry and translations of the great writers of the century and a half that followed, Dryden and Pope and Thomson in particular, have few committed readers today, though they are the very writers we most need to correct us as writers and readers, to restore a balance fatally disturbed by the nineteenth century. Still, their language and forms, quite as much as their concerns, seem remote. Readers who are impatient and un-instructed dismiss what they see as the hubris of poets with so clear a sense of role, so defined a sense of audience, and so restricted – in contemporary terms – a programme.

The hubris, of course, attaches to our age, which rejects as if by reflex the challenge of alien, erudite, and accomplished forebears. Thomas Chatterton is no longer a poet but a case history, the subject for a novel. We love Christopher Smart – if we read him at all – as much for his madness as his poetry. We turn first to the *Jubilate Agno* (usually to 'my Cat Jeffrey', which Benjamin Britten popularized in his wonderful setting) rather than the 'Song to David', prosodically (and spiritually) one of the great poems in the language. He seems, through madness, to escape a cage; we take his escape as *relevant*, that word which brings strange work down to our size, making it familiar and

114

close, and leads to ambitious misreadings. The quality of Blake or Clare is distorted by what modern readers take for freedom – the freedom of an elaborate and subjective mysticism, or of a vision so focused as to issue in madness. Yet it is hard to think of two poets more steeped in certain traditions, more eager to establish legitimacy by reference to forebears.

Some critics and poets writing in America and the Commonwealth as well as in Britain insist that British poets – and we might extend this to include readers – are hamstrung by tradition and convention. Some distinguished Caribbean writers claim that the iambic pentameter is a colonial instrument distorting the natural cadences of native Caribbean English speech. Such views – which are not preposterous – have one virtue: they grant the language of poetry an extraordinary centrality, they insist upon its cultural force. Yet what follows from this, as from the idea that tradition leaves us hamstrung on our native soil, is not that we should avoid tradition and cultivate an ignorance of it in order to start afresh, but rather that we should come to terms with it and master it. It is no accident that the Caribbean critics who advance the theory of iambic colonialism are themselves conversant with the traditions they find distortingly dominant. Had they not mastered those traditions and written some of their best work within them, they would never have been vouchsafed such a vivid, if doubtful, cultural insight. It would be as well to argue that English poetry (not only in Britain) is hamstrung by ignorance of its traditions and conventions, so that we misread originality in the most derivative work, and conventionality in work which revives traditional energy. There ought to be a limit to the number of times the wheel can be invented.

A weak historical sense makes much contemporary poetry seem different in kind from the poetries of the past. This has to do – as we have seen – with the ways in which it is produced, published, and promoted, and the conditions in which it is received. It is the reception of poetry by readers that most interests me in this essay, and yet it is difficult to consider the reader apart from the conditions which solicit his interest and the way in which the poems arrive in printed form before him.

15

There are the Alps. What is there to say about
   them?
They don't make sense. Fatal glaciers, crags cranks
   climb,
jumbled boulder and weed, pasture and boulder,
   scree,
et l'on entend, maybe, *le refrain joyeux et leger.*
Who knows what the ice will have scraped on the
   rock it is smoothing?

There they are, you will have to go a long way
   round
if you want to avoid them.
It takes some getting used to. There are the Alps,
fools! Sit down and wait for them to crumble.

   Basil Bunting, 'On the Fly-Leaf of Pound's *Cantos'*

The greatest reader in the world? Well, the *exemplary* reader of our
century, to go no further back, is Ezra Pound. Pound and the
early Eliot, some teachers insist, remain more 'modern', more
stimulating, exciting, and controversial with young readers,
than any of their successors. Though their work is studied –
selectively, of course, for English readers are generally taken no
further than *Mauberley* in the classroom, and Eliot is diminished
for consumption in various ways – they have not been
assimilated in Britain.

Indeed they keep occasioning controversy. During the 1960s
they seemed to fade; in the 1970s Pound became big business;
in the 1980s their enemies have surfaced once more and
biographies and selective exposées of their lives command more
interest now than their writings do. Yet they refuse to allow
themselves to be reduced to literary history. Their work
continues to stand apart, to challenge and reward us differently

as the years pass and our own *fin de siècle* approaches. Were they not themselves born out of the last effete *fin de siècle*, a period of technical experimentation and exchange, but having lost some essential ingredient, some necessary energies? Pound and Eliot teach us in different ways *how to read* the past and the present.

C. H. Sisson wrote in 1949, at a time when Pound's credit was low:

> If one remembers, after eighteen years, the time, the weather and the exact place of one's first encounter with the work of a particular writer, it is safe to say that that writer produced an initial effect. If, after that time, one is still reading him with pleasure as well as admiration, it may be that the total effect has been one of those real adjustments of mind which even the most omnivorous reader can expect from only a few writers. (*The Avoidance of Literature*: 76)

It is worth dwelling on the phrase, 'one of those real adjustments of mind'. The poetry, in its rhythms and diction, its tonal changes and (lastly) its 'meanings', effected a change in an attentive reader, quite a radical change. Sisson also owed a long-standing debt to Pound's *ABC of Reading*. It may be that his encounter with Pound did more to emancipate Sisson than any other experience he has had as a writer. He was freed not into imitation of Pound, but from imitation of other models. A sense of active tradition replaced a sense of acceptable convention. Eliot had prepared Sisson for Pound, and the debt to Eliot is sometimes audible in Sisson's own rhythms; yet the abiding debt, the radical debt is to Pound. Pound had, at rather closer range, just such an effect on Eliot himself.

Introducing his translation of the *Anabase* of St-Jean Perse, Eliot borrows comments from Emile Fabré, comments which can be usefully transposed into the context of this essay. Obscurities in Perse's poem on first reading are due, he says, to the suppression of 'links in the chain', passages of explanation and transition, 'narrative', and not to imaginative confusion or a desire to obscure meaning. We are familiar with such suppressions in the early work of Eliot, in Pound, in David

Jones's *Anathemata*, Basil Bunting's *Briggflatts*, C. H. Sisson's 'The Usk' and 'In Insula Avalonia', Donald Davie's *Three for Watermusic* and Geoffrey Hill's 'Pentecost Castle', among other works.

Fabré argues that in Perse's poem the abbreviated form compacts the matter into an impression of barbaric civilization, a judgement with which one may disagree without letting the suggestion go. Readers, Fabré insists, must learn to allow the images to fall into memory (here memory and imagination become almost inseparable) as they come, without interrogating whether they are 'reasonable' image by image. 'There is a logic of the imagination as well as a logic of concepts.' Fabré does not say that these two logics are necessarily exclusive of one another – they may overlap, they may coincide, and yet they must be discriminated because they are different in kind.

The logic of the imagination expressed as rhythms that allow *lacunae* and syncopation in the progression of imagery and argument, elision in the development of tone and mood, characterizes some of the noblest poetry of our century, and not only poetry in English. Penetrating the logic of imagination of different poems (one cannot accurately say of different poets, since each poem has a different dynamic) is a skill the reader can and the critic must acquire.

This logic of imagination is inextricable from the structure of different languages as used by specific writers at specific times. Pound has no peer in his choice of dictions in translation, and in his sense of the kinds of irony and innocence attributable to the voices of the poet translated, given period, theme, and subject. Where a Victorian translator, like the excellent Edward Fitzgerald, while loving the foreignness of his texts assimilated them into the conventions that were second nature to him, so that his *Rubaiyat* is a high-point of Victorian poetry, Pound sets out to establish what was different in his, to give them their own characteristics within the limitations of the English he had. He sets the translator a radical challenge, and gives the reader invaluable resources.

What sets his *Cantos* apart is their acute differentiation of dictions and registers of language, so that the juxtaposition of phrases or longer passages from distinct cultures, the imitations and parodies, the interplay between different demotic usages and highly literary usages, the contrast between prose and poetry, require of us the cultivation of an active imagination and, more than that, a sense of history – the history of our language, and of the otherness of other periods, languages, and cultures. The more we hear, the more we sense how integration in Pound's work comes, not in despite of his rigorous differentiations but because of them. The musical analogy comes to mind: the sudden modulation from one register to another, from one diction or frame of allusion to another, is comparable in emotional and intellectual impact to a key change in music. The resonance of the *Pisan Cantos* in particular is in the essential thrift of allusions, those little vortices which define periods of cultural fruition and the prose centuries that separate them, the interchange between the logic of concepts and the logic of imagination. Pound insists on reading – on hearing – the past and the alien in its own terms, and he refuses to acclimatize or assimilate them into a false contemporary coherence.

The reader of modern poetry could do worse than begin – or begin again – with Pound and Eliot. Not with criticisms of their work, but with the poetry, prose, and translations themselves. There are other places to start from and other places to go, but in the end there is no way around them.

Reading list

This list of anthologies, critical books and collections is strictly abbreviated and selective. I indicate where *Selected* and *Collected* editions exist. Otherwise the author's name is followed by 'various titles', to indicate a generalized interest in his or her work, to be pursued through a range of separate collections. Publishers are in London unless otherwise stated.

Anthologies

Fleur Adcock, *Faber Book of Twentieth-Century Women's Poetry* (1987)

A. Crozier and T. Longville, *A Various Art* (Manchester: 1988)

D.J. Enright, *The Oxford Book of Contemporary Verse* (1980)

B. Morrison and A. Motion, *New English Poetry* (Harmondsworth: 1984)

Michael Roberts, *The Faber Book of Modern Verse* (1940)

Michael Schmidt, *Eleven British Poets* (1981)

———— *Some Contemporary Poets* (Manchester: 1985)

Geoffrey Summerfield, *Worlds: Seven Modern Poets* (Harmondsworth: 1974)

David Wright, *X Anthology* (Oxford: 1988)

Criticism and essays

George Barker, *Essays* (1970)

Samuel Taylor Coleridge, *Biographia Literaria* (Everyman edn: 1965)

Donald Davie, *Articulate Energy* (1955)

———— *Czeslaw Milosz and the Insufficiency of the Lyric* (1985)

———— *Purity of Diction in English Verse* (1952)

———— *The Poet in the Imaginary Museum* (1977)

—— *Thomas Hardy and British Poetry* (1973)
—— *Under Briggflatts* (1989)
Thom Gunn, *The Occasions of Poetry* (1983)
Michael Hamburger, *The Truth of Poetry* (1969)
David Jones, *Epoch and Artist* (1958)
P. Jones and M. Schmidt, *British Poetry since 1970* (Cheadle Hulme: 1973)
Christopher Middleton, *Bolshevism in Art* (Manchester: 1971)
—— *The Pursuit of the Kingfisher* (Manchester: 1983)
Edgell Rickword, *Essays and Opinions 1921–1931* (Cheadle Hulme: 1974)
—— *Literature in Society* (Manchester: 1980)
—— *Scrutinies of Various Writers* (London: 1928)
C.H. Sisson, *The Avoidance of Literature* (Manchester: 1978)
—— *English Poetry 1900–1950* (1971)
Allen Tate, *Essays of Four Decades* (Oxford: 1970)
Yvor Winters, *Forms of Discovery* (Denver: 1967)
—— *The Function of Criticism* (Denver: 1957)

Poets and poetry

John Ash, various titles
John Ashbery, *Selected Poems* (Manchester: 1986)
Cliff Ashby, *Plain Song: Collected Poems* (Manchester: 1985)
George Barker, *Collected Poems* (1986)
James K. Baxter, *Collected Poems* (Oxford: 1982)
Patricia Beer, *Collected Poems* (Manchester: 1988)
Sir John Betjeman, *Collected Poems* (1984)
Elizabeth Bishop, *The Complete Poems* (1983)
Eavan Boland, *Selected Poems* (Manchester: 1989)
Alison Brackenbury, various titles
Basil Bunting, *Collected Poems* (Oxford: 1978)
Charles Causley, *Collected Poems* (1975)
Gillian Clarke, *Selected Poems* (Manchester: 1985)
David Constantine, various titles
Hart Crane (ed. B. Weber), *Complete Poems and Selected Letters* (Oxford: 1968)
Anthony Cronin, *New and Selected Poems* (Manchester: 1983)

Elizabeth Daryush, *Collected Poems* (Cheadle Hulme: 1976)
Donald Davie, *Collected Poems 1950–1970* (1972)
——— *Collected Poems 1971–1983* (1984)
Dick Davis, *Devices and Desires* (1989)
Alistair Elliot, *Collected Poems* (Manchester: 1989)
D.J. Enright, *Collected Poems* (Oxford: 1981)
James Fenton, *The Memory of War* (1984)
Roy Fuller, *Collected Poems* (1962)
W.S. Graham, *Collected Poems* (1980)
Thom Gunn, various titles
Michael Hamburger, *Collected Poems* (Manchester: 1982)
Tony Harrison, *Selected Poems* (Harmondsworth: 1982)
Seamus Heaney, various titles
John Heath-Stubbs, *Collected Poems* (Manchester: 1988)
Geoffrey Hill, *Collected Poems* (1985)
Michael Hofmann, various titles
Jeremy Hooker, *A View from the Source* (Manchester: 1982)
A.D. Hope, *Selected Poems* (Manchester: 1986)
Ted Hughes, various titles
Daniel Huws, *Noth* (1972)
Elizabeth Jennings, *Collected Poems* (Manchester: 1986)
Brian Jones, various titles
David Jones, various titles
Patrick Kavanagh, *Collected Poems* (1972)
Philip Larkin, *Collected Poems* (1987)
Wyndham Lewis, *Collected Poems and Plays* (Manchester: 1979)
Robert Lowell, *Selected Poems* (1969)
Norman MacCaig, *Selected Poems* (1971)
Hugh MacDiarmid, *Collected Poems* (1984)
Derek Mahon, various titles
Christopher Middleton, *111 Poems* (Manchester: 1983)
Edwin Morgan, *Poems of Thirty Years* (Manchester: 1982)
——— *Selected Poems* (Manchester: 1985)
Andrew Motion, *Dangerous Play* (1984)
Les A. Murray, *Selected Poems* (Manchester: 1986)
Tom Paulin, various titles
Sylvia Plath, *Collected Poems* (1986)
J.H. Prynne, *Poems* (1984)

Rodney Pybus, *Cicadas in their Summers* (Manchester: 1988)
Edgell Rickword, *Behind the Eyes: Collected Poems* (Manchester: 1973)
John Riley, *The Collected Works* (1981)
Carol Rumens, various titles
Peter Sansom, *Poems* (Manchester: 1990)
E.J. Scovell, *Collected Poems* (Manchester: 1988)
Peter Scupham, various titles
Burns Singer, *Selected Poems* (Manchester: 1977)
C.H. Sisson, *Collected Poems* (Manchester: 1984)
—————— *Selected Poems* (Manchester: 1981)
Ken Smith, various titles
Iain Crichton Smith, *Selected Poems* (Manchester: 1985)
Stevie Smith, *Collected Poems* (1975)
R.S. Thomas, *Selected Poems* (1973)
Charles Tomlinson, *Collected Poems* (Oxford: 1984)
Jeffrey Wainwright, *Selected Poems* (Manchester: 1985)
Derek Walcott, *Collected Poems* (1988)
Val Warner, various titles
Robert Wells, *Selected Poems* (Manchester: 1986)
David Wright, *Selected Poems* (Manchester: 1988)

Name index